William Hewson

Illustrations of Tracts on the Greek-Egyptian Sun-Dial With Seven Steps

Being the second and third series of illustrations for Tracts on Christianity in its relation to Judaism and heathenism

William Hewson

Illustrations of Tracts on the Greek-Egyptian Sun-Dial With Seven Steps
Being the second and third series of illustrations for Tracts on Christianity in its relation to Judaism and heathenism

ISBN/EAN: 9783337243210

Printed in Europe, USA, Canada, Australia, Japan

Cover: Foto ©Lupo / pixelio.de

More available books at **www.hansebooks.com**

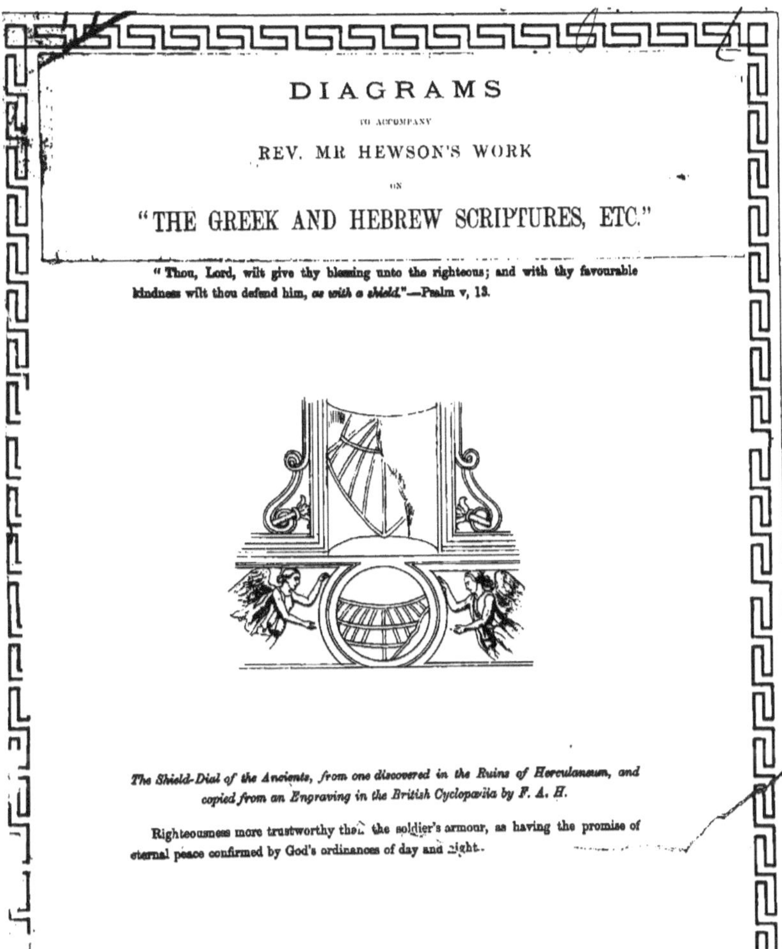

DIAGRAMS

TO ACCOMPANY

REV. MR HEWSON'S WORK

ON

"THE GREEK AND HEBREW SCRIPTURES, ETC."

"Thou, Lord, wilt give thy blessing unto the righteous; and with thy favourable kindness wilt thou defend him, *as with a shield*."—Psalm v, 13.

The Shield-Dial of the Ancients, from one discovered in the Ruins of Herculaneum, and copied from an Engraving in the British Cyclopædia by F. A. H.

Righteousness more trustworthy than the soldier's armour, as having the promise of eternal peace confirmed by God's ordinances of day and night.

ILLUSTRATIONS OF TRACTS

ON THE

GREEK-EGYPTIAN SUN-DIAL, WITH SEVEN STEPS, ETC.:

BEING THE

SECOND AND THIRD SERIES OF ILLUSTRATIONS

FOR

TRACTS ON CHRISTIANITY IN ITS RELATION TO
JUDAISM AND HEATHENISM, ETC. ETC.

BY THE LATE

REV. WILLIAM HEWSON, M.A.,

VICAR OF GOATHLAND.

LONDON:

SIMPKIN & CO., STATIONERS' HALL COURT; SEELEYS, FLEET STREET; HATCHARD, PICCADILLY;
NISBET, BERNERS STREET. WHITBY: HORNE & SON. WIGTON: M'MECHAN.
EDINBURGH: W. OLIPHANT & CO.; ANDREW ELLIOT.

1870.

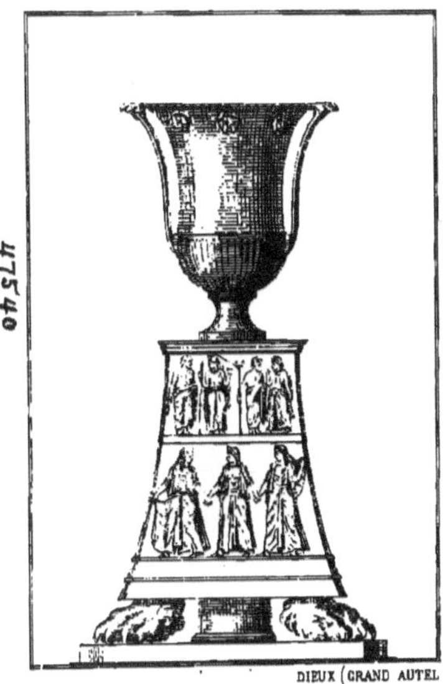

DIEUX (GRAND AUTEL DES DOUZE)

THE OLD YEAR OF 3 SEASONS COMPARED WITH THE MONTH OF 3 WEEKS
FROM A SCULPTURE IN THE LOUVRE, AT PARIS

CONTINUATION OF THE DESIGNS ON THE BEFOREMENTIONED SCULPTURE

The Indian Zodiac.

OF THE *ENCYCLOPEDIA LONDINENSIS.*

Comparing the weekly Cycle of nine days (as that of the Romans in the days of Horace), with the Solar Cycle of 12 × 30 = 360 days.

This, compared with the week of seven days, represents the combat between the three Horatii against the three Curiatii as a conflict between the Nodes of ascending and descending light, until leaving, from the week of nine days, only six to the Planets and one to the Sun.

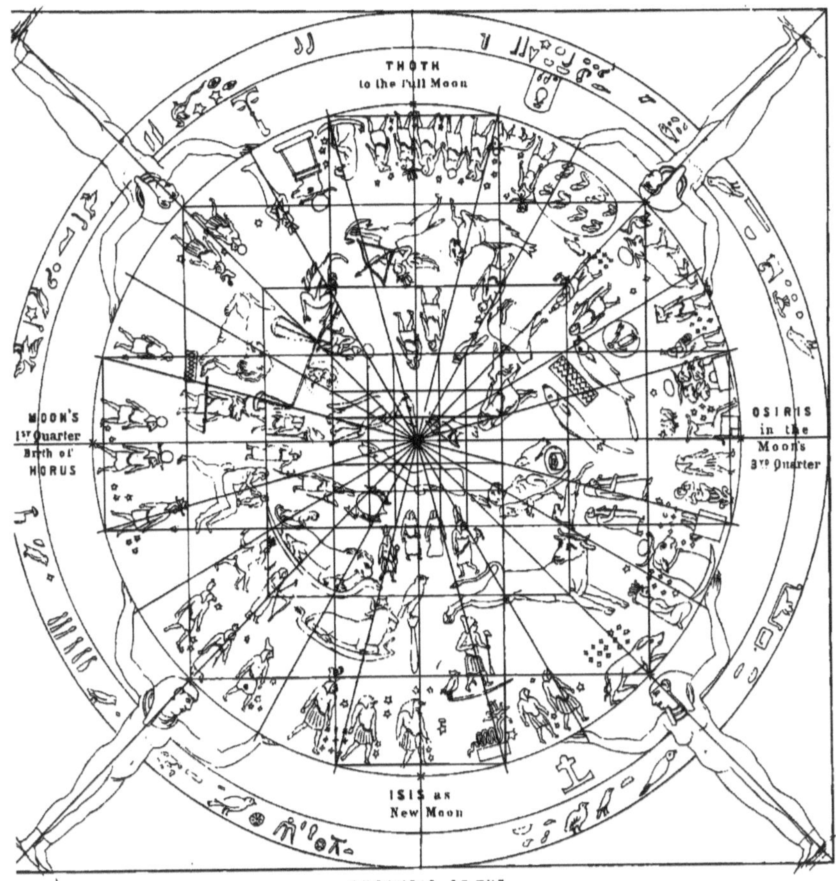

ANALYSIS OF THE

Planisphere taken from the Temple of Tentyra

Symbolising the relation of the Circle to the Square; as "*the Island*" of the Mysteries, "*with a strong door and quadrilateral inclosure.*"

Compare Faber's *Origin of Idolatry*, vol. ii, p. 167, with the *four*-furrowed inclosure *sacred to Mars*, which Jason ploughed with fire-breathing bulls, and sowed with dragon's teeth.—*Apollonius Rhodius*, lib. iii, v. 1344-1358. The Cycle of the Solar year in its relation to their diurnal arc, on the east and west dialling of the ancients.

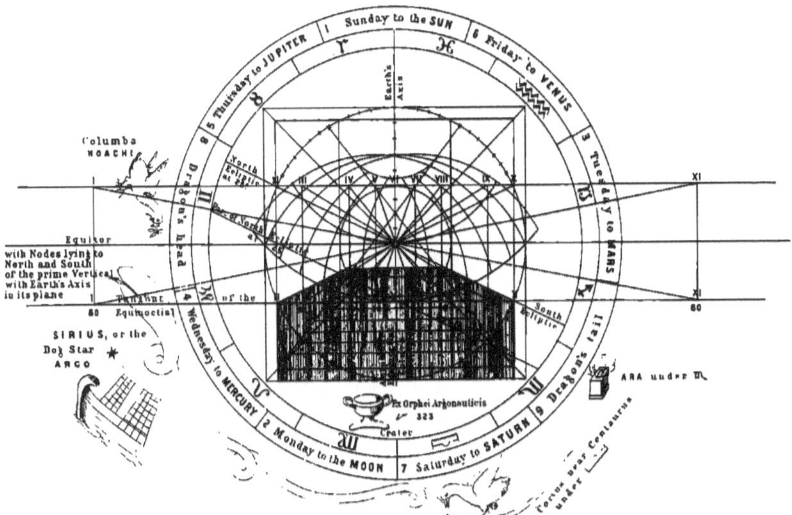

The days of the week are here given to the signs of the zodiac as on the Indian zodiac in the *Encyclopedia Londinensis*, which seemingly refers to the oldest solar year of three seasons in its relation to their east and west dialling. For that gave the western hemisphere to *the north, for the zenith of the dial*, and the eastern hemisphere to the south, *for its nadir; when the north was given to God, and the south* (*as a draught house*, 2 Kings x, 29, in the dragon symbolism for the nodes—compared with the late Emperor of China's Jos), to the lower regions of this typical instruction respecting the true light of man's life in God, as revealed under a mystery of godliness (*i.e.*, under a mystery of the divine and human nature combined in Christ).

Diagram for the Oldest Year of three Seasons, and the division of the Earth to the three Sons of Noah.

1 The Sun beginning his diurnal arc, and weekly circuit of nine days, from Jupiter, as then turning from his third western gate to rise in his *third* eastern gate with Hercules, for the beginning of his twelve labours, descending from between his Nodes.

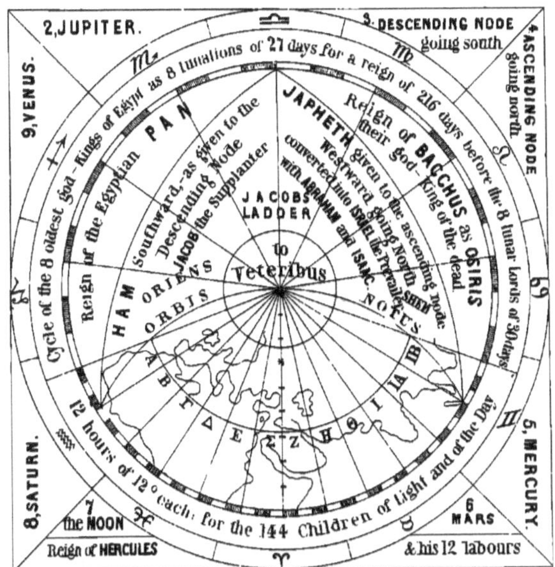

The East and West Dialling of the Orientals.

This harmonises the Egyptian and Hindu zodiacs with the relation of the Noah's ark symbolism to that of the 144 children of the light and of the day, as typically numbered by *thousands* over Israel.—Rev. vii, xiv.

Compare also its relation to the division of the whole earth between the three sons of Noah after the flood.

The prime vertical of the dial is here supposed to pass through Ur of the Chaldees.

EAST AND WEST FACES OF THE GREEK-EGYPTIAN DIAL WITH STEPS.

The Hindu Zodiac for the week of eight days, beginning from Jupiter (or between Thursday and Friday), given to the morning hours of an East Dial for N. lat. 25°, on the east face of the Greek-Egyptian Dial with steps.

The relation of the square to the circle in this figure forms the basis of a typical comparison between the old year of three seasons and ours of four seasons. Thus the inner and symmetrical square of Professor Piazzi Smyth proves the source of the metaphor under which the New Jerusalem is spoken of in Revelations—as the city of God's kingdom of light—coming down from heaven "*four square*."

The Hindu Zodiac for the week of nine days (whence ours of seven days, as 7 × 40° symbolised to the old lunar year of 10 × 28 days), given to the afternoon hours of a West Dial for N. lat. 25°, on the west face of the Greek-Egyptian Dial with Steps.

The relation of the square to the circle (which obviously forms the basis of this dialling) will, I hope, tend to confirm that idea of a typical design in the Pyramid building which Professor Piazzi Smyth seems to have traced astronomically.

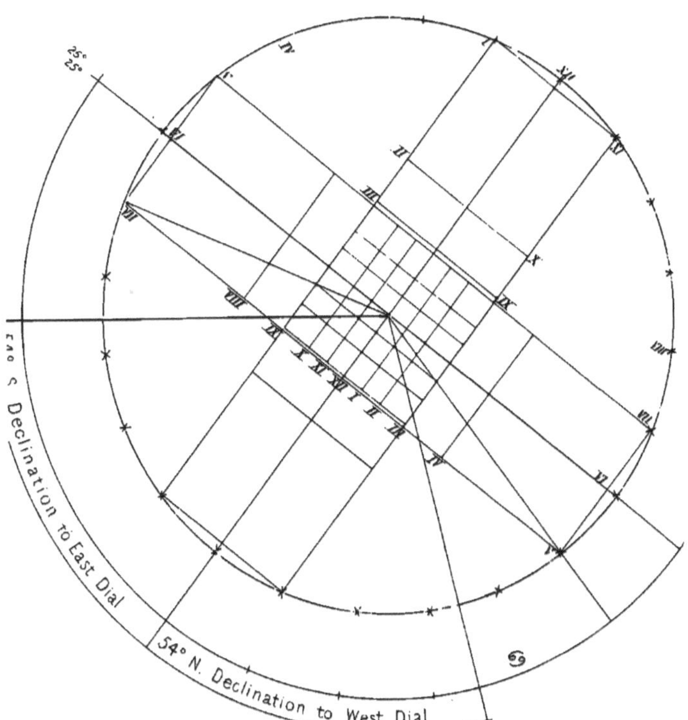

The Equator and Earth's Axis, as marked above, refer to the shaded outline of the Hollow Dial with Steps. But Ferguson's Quadrant Card Dial places Earth's Axis, and base of the Trigon, on the hour of VI., giving that of XII. to the Equator. It will be necessary to bear this in mind, when adjusting the plumb-line on the Card Dial to the day of the month on the Analemma, which is rightly placed on the hour of VI.

* *Perhaps I ought to have said a Polar Dial, seeing that it stands on the hour of XII. For Earth's Axis is numbered to the VIth hour on an East or West Dial. In each case, however, its elevation above the horizon is equal to the latitude of the place, as here marked.*

The Symbolic Structure of the Great Pyramid, compared with that of the Greek-Egyptian Dial with Steps.

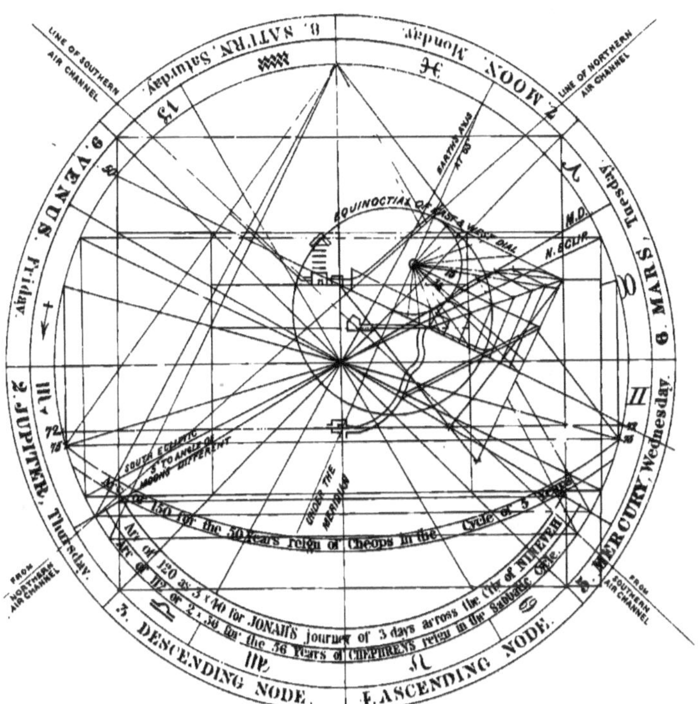

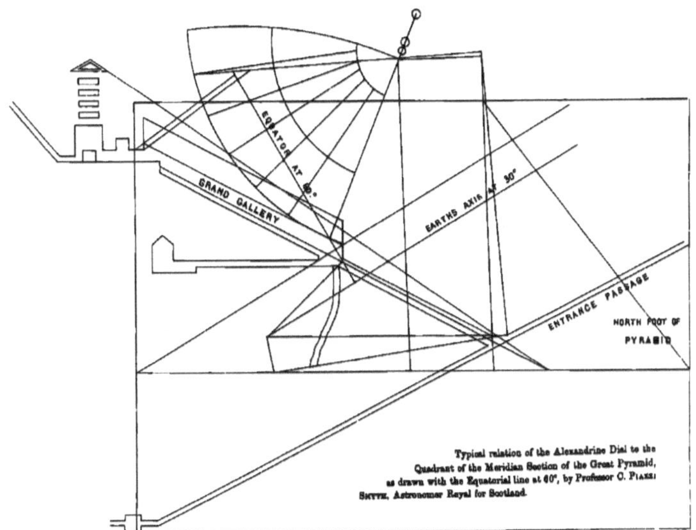

Typical relation of the Alexandrine Dial to the Quadrant of the Meridian Section of the Great Pyramid, as drawn with the Equatorial line at 60°, by Professor C. Piazzi Smyth, Astronomer Royal for Scotland.

The Greek Egyptian Dial, with Steps, in its probable relation to a Typical Design in the Pyramid Building. Compare with this Symbolism the Metaphor of Rev. xii. 1, xix. 17, as contrasting the Advent of the Sun of Righteousness with a darkening of the Heavens of the then dominant Idolatry of Baalism.

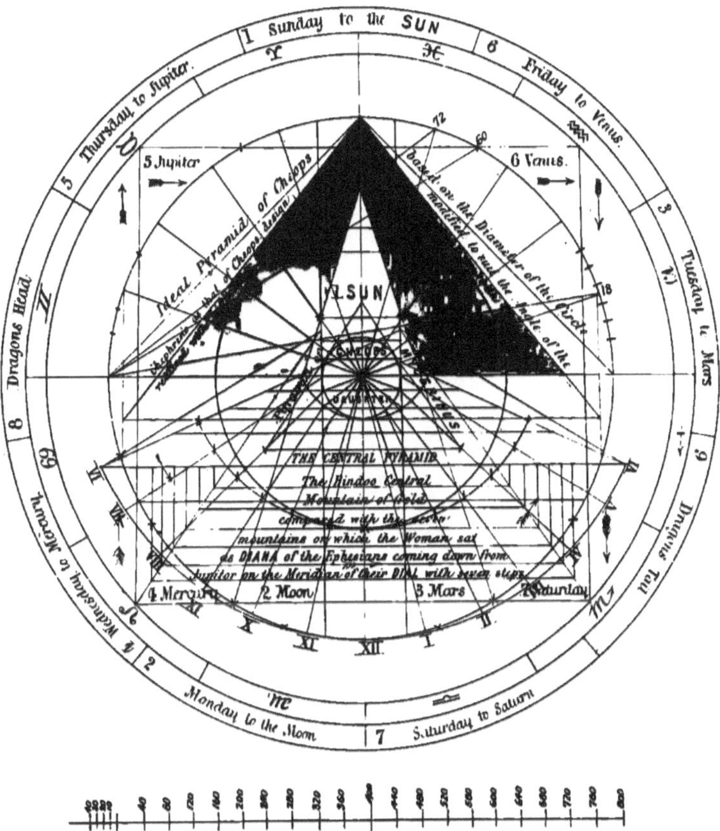

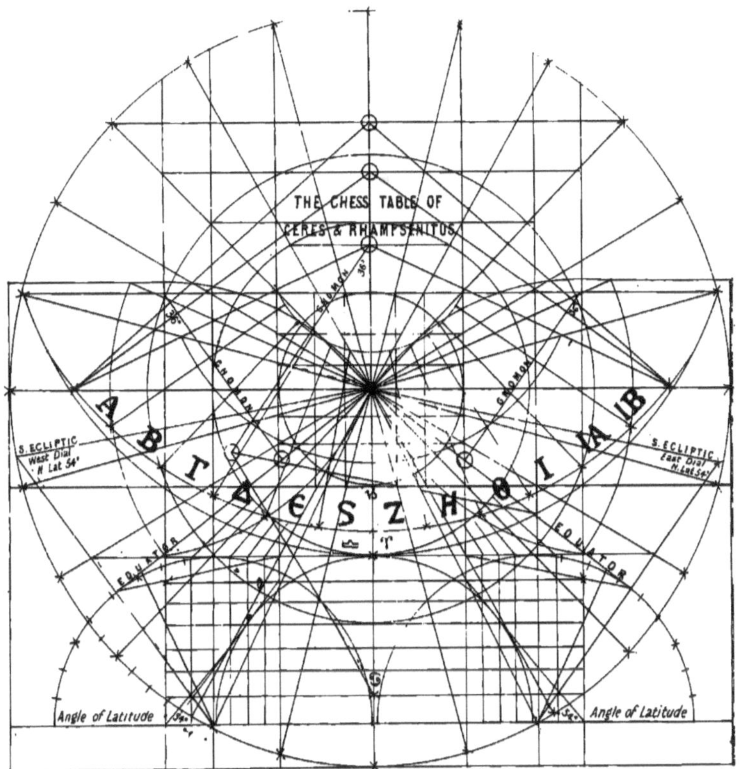
THE CHESS TABLE OF
CERES & RHAMPSENITUS
GNOMON 36°
GNOMON
GNOMON
S. ECLIPTIC
West Dial
N Lat 54°
S. ECLIPTIC
East Dial
N. Lat 54°
EQUATOR
EQUATOR
Α Β Γ Δ Є S Ζ Η Θ Ι ΙΑ ΙΒ
Angle of Latitude
Angle of Latitude

The Typical Structure of the Great Pyramid, as a Symbolism from the East and West Dialling of the Ancient Orientals; also for the Full Moon between her nodes, when lying north and south. *See* "Colman's Hindu Mythology."

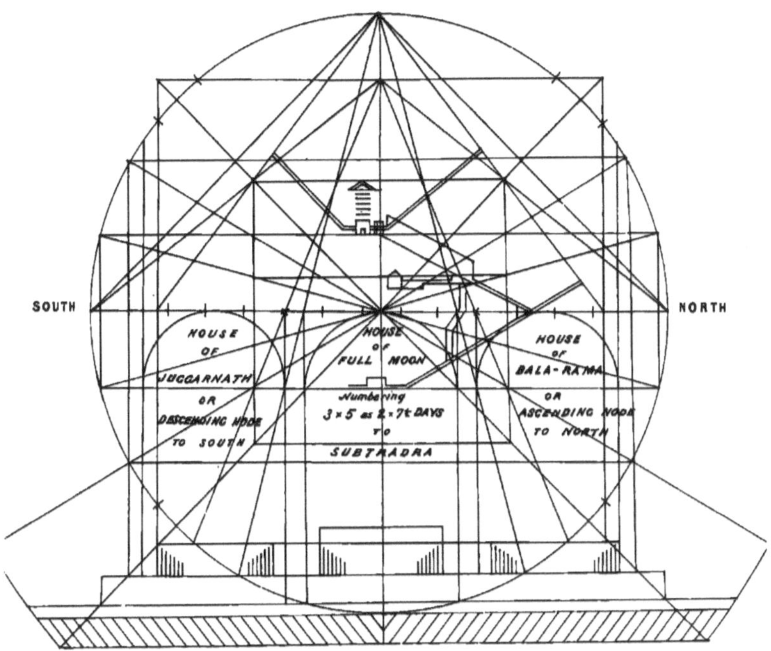

Compare Luke xii. 52, on the house of five divided against itself, as by the typical worshippers of God, according to the law of His Sabbaths, against the idolators and their cycle of five years.

THE PYRAMID SYMBOLISM

Adapted to the structure of the Alexandrine or Greek-Egyptian Dial with Steps (considered as an Upper Inclined East Dial for N. lat. 65, with angle of inclination 30°), on the scale of the model made from the original by Mr A. Hayes of the British Museum.

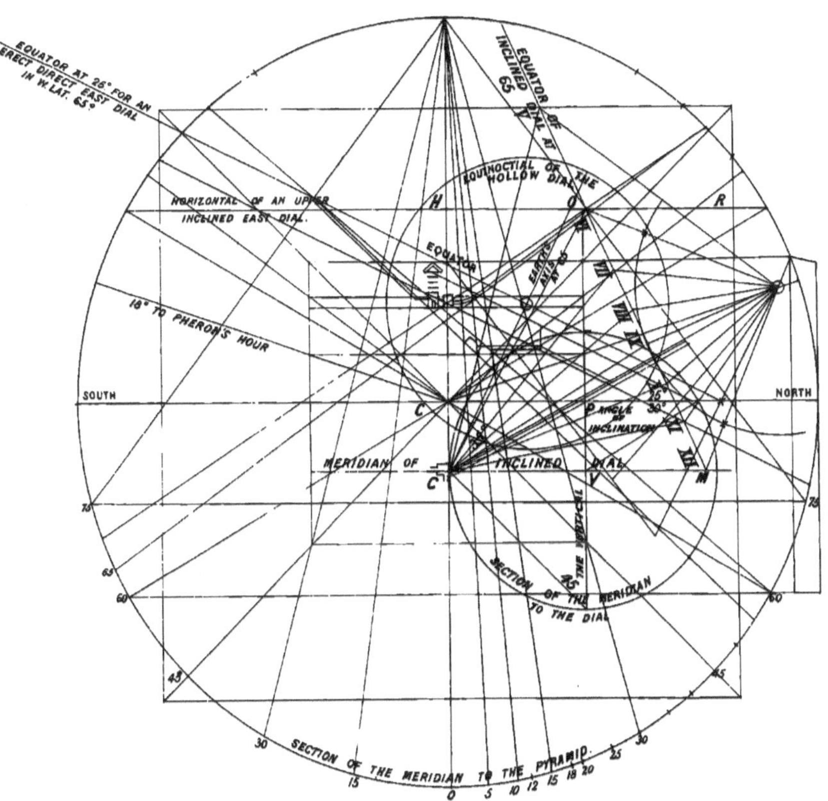

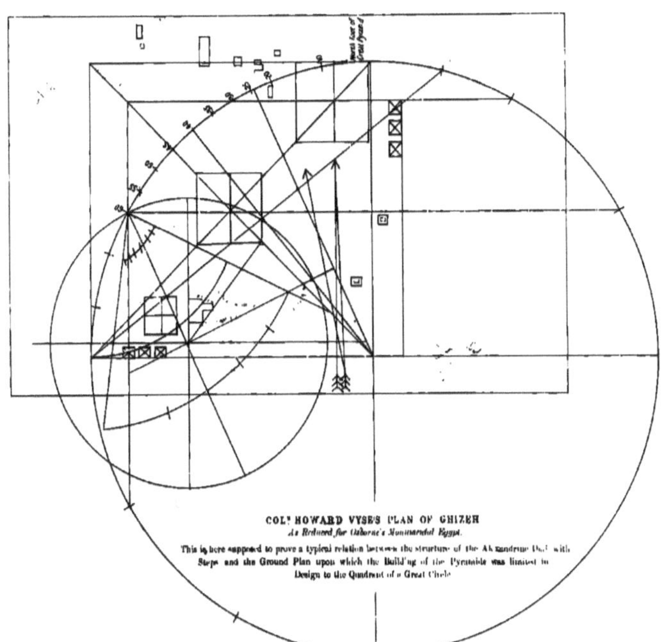

COL. HOWARD VYSE'S PLAN OF GHIZEH

As Reduced for Osborne's Monumental Egypt.

This is here supposed to prove a typical relation between the structure of the Alexandrine Dial with Steps and the Ground Plan upon which the Building of the Pyramids was limited in Design to the Quadrant of a Great Circle

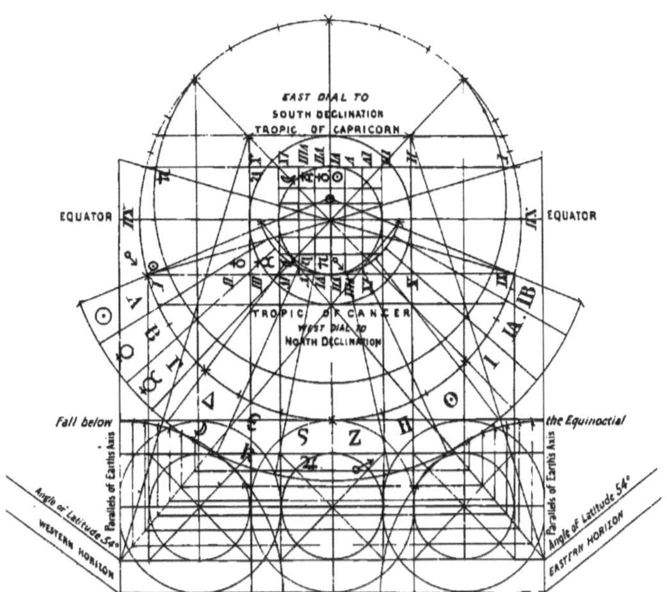

THE DIAGRAM REFERRED TO IN CONCLUDING REMARKS.

Compare the squares described about the three small circles on the steps, with the three small Pyramids between the same parallels in the plain of Ghizeh.

Fig. 1.—Quadrant of the Great Pyramid, with the three small Pyramids (of which the central one is that of Cheops' daughter) on its eastern side.

This forms a symbolism for the diurnal arc on an East and West Dial (compared with the Quadrant Dial of the Egyptians), given to the Moon between her nodes.

Fig. 2.—The *third* Pyramid, or that of Mycerinus, with other *three* small Pyramids between the same parallels, on its southern front.

This forms a symbolism for the diurnal arc of an East and West (compared with a Horizontal) Dial, given to the Moon between her nodes. As to "the head and tail of the dragon," by which the Orientals meant the intersection of two circles,—viz., that of the Ecliptic by the Moon's orbit,—see Blundevil, as quoted in page 5 of my Notes on APHOPHIS. (Compare the *penthouse roof, with its double apex*, in the symbolic idol of Subhadra, between her two brothers, Juggarnath and Bala Rama, as copied from Coleman's Hindu-Mythology.) These symbolisms show how the Orientals anciently divided the week of seven days, between ascending and descending light, to the diurnal arc of ten hours, on the stems of their ancient dialling with steps, as may be seen in the structure of the Alexandrine or Greek Egyptian Dial with Steps.

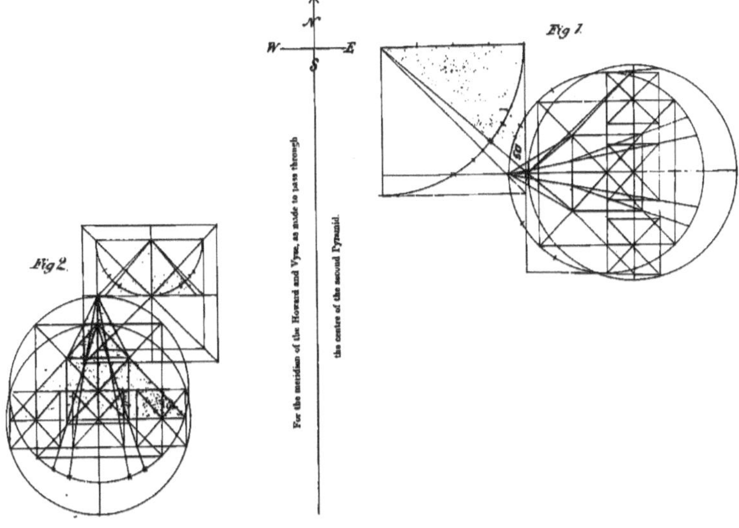

Mr George Thurnell's problem, respecting the measurement of the Great Pyramid, applied to the structure of the Greek Egyptian Dial, with steps, *on its eastern face.*

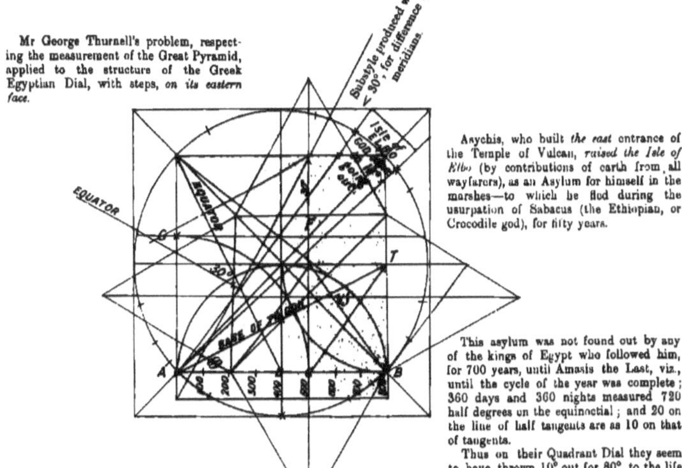

Asychis, who built *the east* entrance of the Temple of Vulcan, *raised the Isle of Elbo* (by contributions of earth from all wayfarers), as an Asylum for himself in the marshes—to which he fled during the usurpation of Sabacus (the Ethiopian, or Crocodile god), for fifty years.

This asylum was not found out by any of the kings of Egypt who followed him, for 700 years, until Amasis the Last, viz., until the cycle of the year was complete; 360 days and 360 nights measured 720 half degrees on the equinoctial; and 20 on the line of half tangents are as 10 on that of tangents.

Thus on their Quadrant Dial they seem to have thrown 10° out for 80°, to the life of APHOPHRIS.

The symbolic design of the Pyramid builders, traced from the measurements recorded by Herodotus.

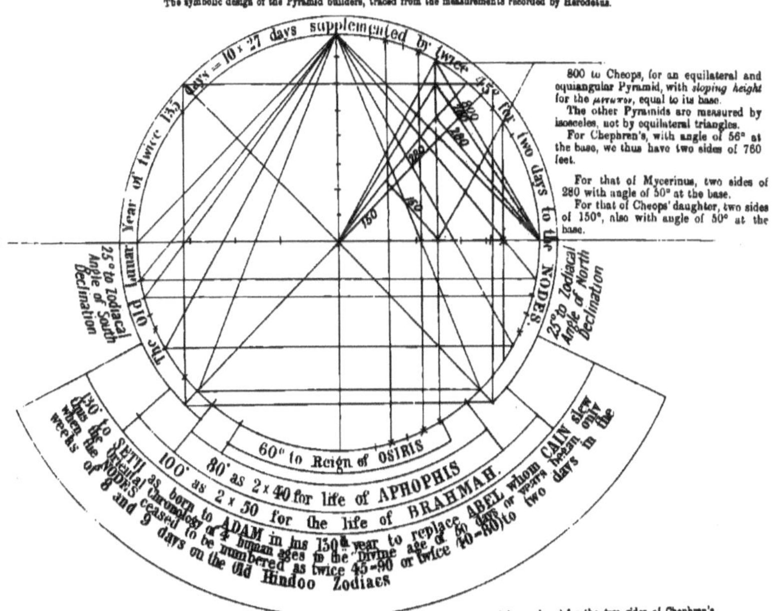

800 to Cheops, for an equilateral and equiangular Pyramid, with *sloping height* for the *μετωπον*, equal to its base.

The other Pyramids are measured by isosceles, not by equilateral triangles.

For Chephren's, with angle of 56° at the base, we thus have two sides of 760 feet.

For that of Mycerinus, two sides of 280 with angle of 50° at the base.

For that of Cheops' daughter, two sides of 150°, also with angle of 50° at the base.

N.B.—This symbolism gives a sloping height of 760 (or 800 less 40, or less by the 40 feet at which it stood lower down) for the two sides of Chephren's [illegible]. Its shape is thus that of an isosceles, not an equilateral triangle, having at the base an angle of 56°, according to the years of his reign.

But if Herodotus meant to say that each triangular face had a sloping side equal to its breadth of base, the form would be that of an equilateral and equiangular triangle, and the measurements for these two Pyramids would stand thus :—

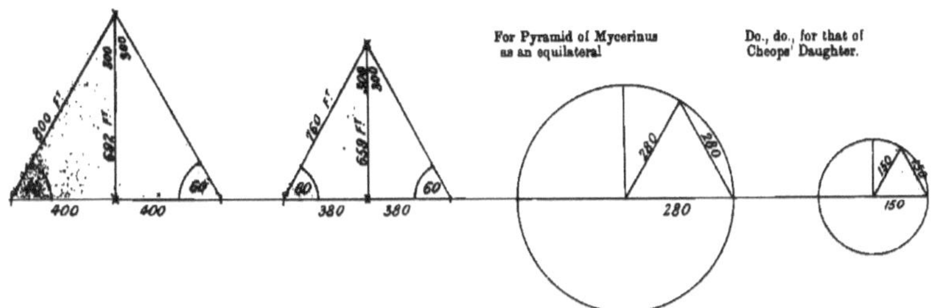

The relation of the Pyramid of Cheops, and his reign of fifty years (with that of Chephren and his reign of fifty-six years), to the equinoctial of the Greek-Egyptian Dial, as a hollow quadrant dial.

Thus the hill on which these two Pyramids were built seems to have symbolised a quadrant of the meridian. Upon such a supposition, we readily perceive a meaning answering to the form of the subjoined diagram. In the words of Herodotus, that the Pyramid of Chephren was built forty feet *lower down on the same hill of one hundred feet high;* and was to some extent (or proportionately) less in size.

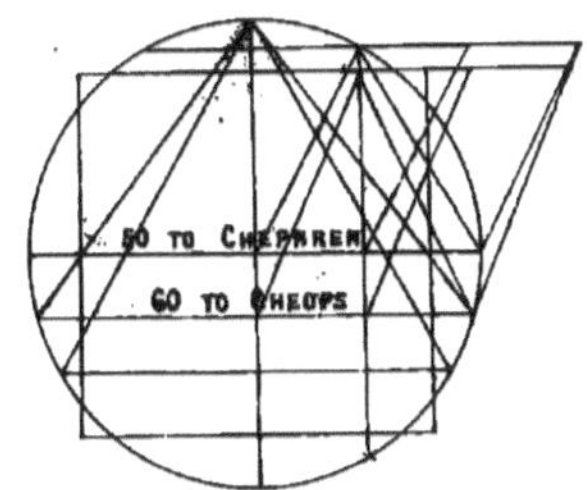

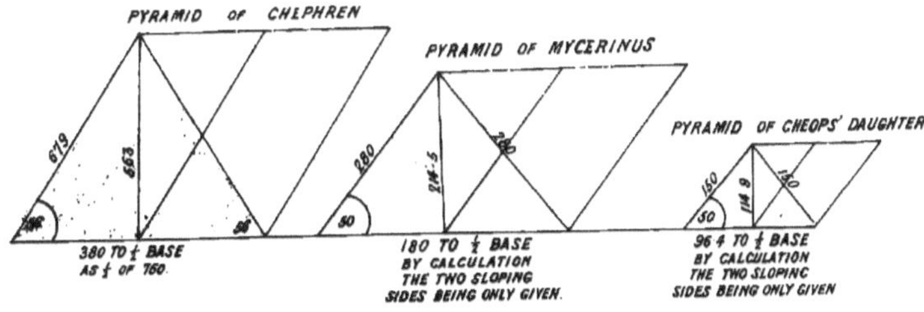

THE TYPICAL FEATURES OF THE EXODUS,

Illustrated by the Structure of the Alexandrine or Greek-Egyptian Dial.

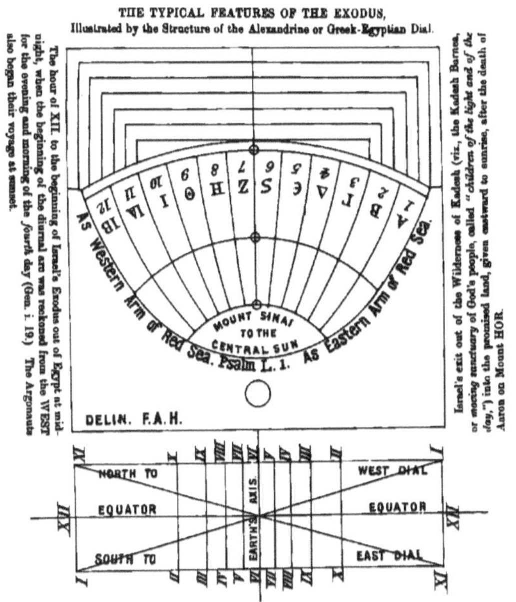

Dialling illustration of the 40 years
DAY of Temptation in the Wilderness.

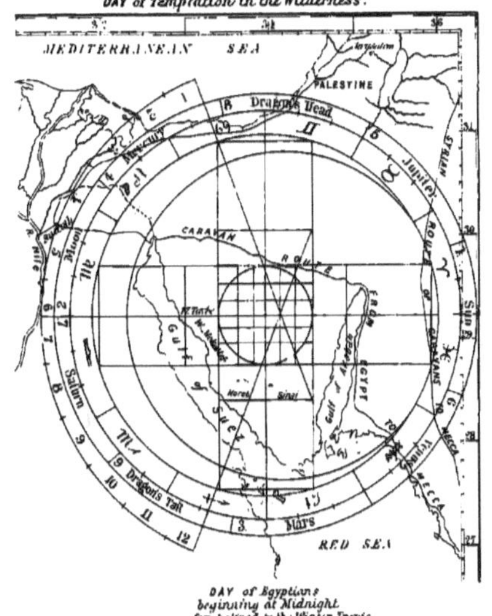

DAY of Egyptians
beginning at Midnight
Symbolized to the Winter Tropic
as the THOTH, or beginning of their Year

Descent of **HERCULES** *into* **HADES**
by the river **ACHERON**

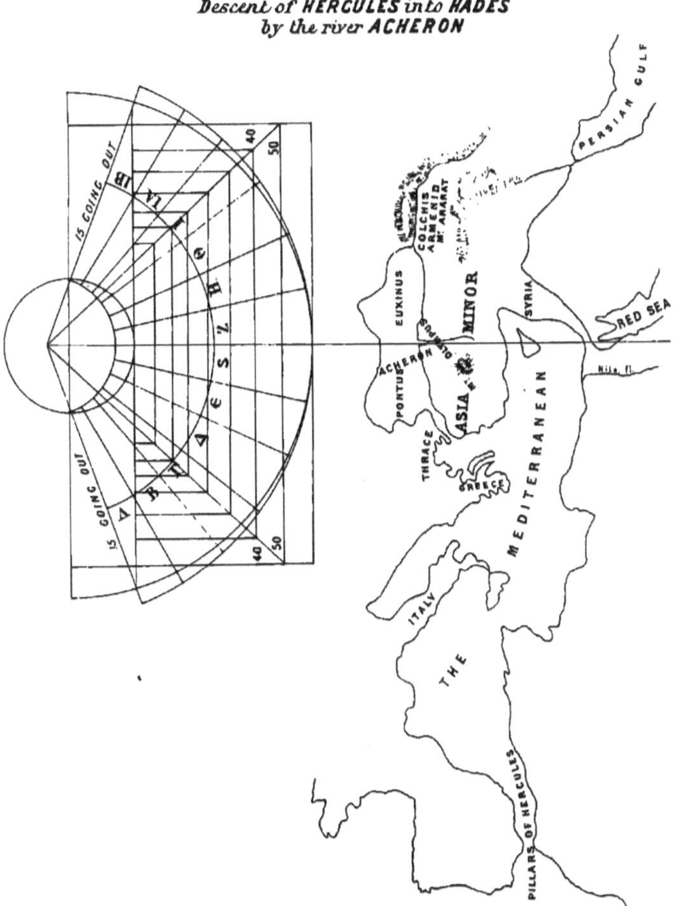

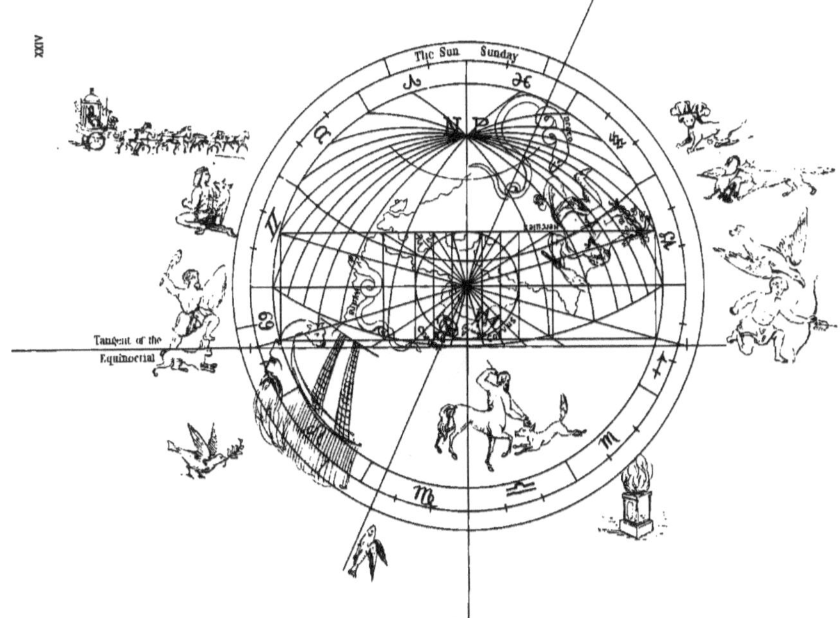
XIX
The Sun
Sunday
N P
Tangent of the
Equinoctial

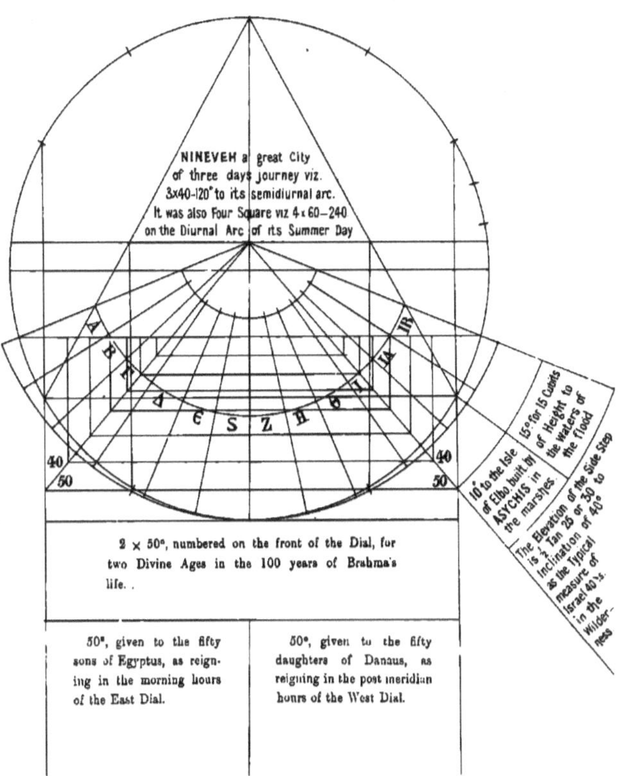

NINEVEH a great City
of three days journey viz.
3x40-120° to its semidiurnal arc.
It was also Four Square viz 4 x 60–240
on the Diurnal Arc of its Summer Day
40
50
40
50
15° for 15 Cubits
of Height to
the waters of
the flood
10° to the Isle
of Elbo built by
ASYCHIS in
the marshes.
2 × 50°, numbered on the front of the Dial, for
two Divine Ages in the 100 years of Brahma's
life.
50°, given to the fifty
sons of Egyptus, as reigning in the morning hours
of the East Dial.
50°, given to the fifty
daughters of Danaus, as
reigning in the post meridian
hours of the West Dial.

N.B.—4 × 60 = 12 × 20 = 240.—For four cycles of OSIRIS, in the eight months of the Summer season, when numbering 8 × 30, instead of 8 × 27 = 216 days, to the reign of the eight oldest gods of Egypt.

4 × 84 = 12 × 28.—For the earliest cycle of the twelve gods who followed the previous eight, and whose reign numbered four cycles of Helius.

4 × 90 = 12 × 30, as 3 × 120.—For the old Chaldean solar year of three seasons, divided to the reigns of PAN, HERCULES, and BACCHUS, by the Egyptians.

The Diurnal Arc on an East and West Dial, variously symbolised to the signs of the Zodiac :

1st.—As returning Eastward from the North, according to Enoch's astronomy.

2d.—As returning Westward from the North. This brings ♌ to the *right* of the Solstitial Colure, as in Ezekiel's Vision of Prophecy respecting heaven as God's throne, cap. i, v. 10. Compare Jonah iv. 11, for the 120.000 souls in NINEVEH, *too ignorant* to discern between their right hand and their left.

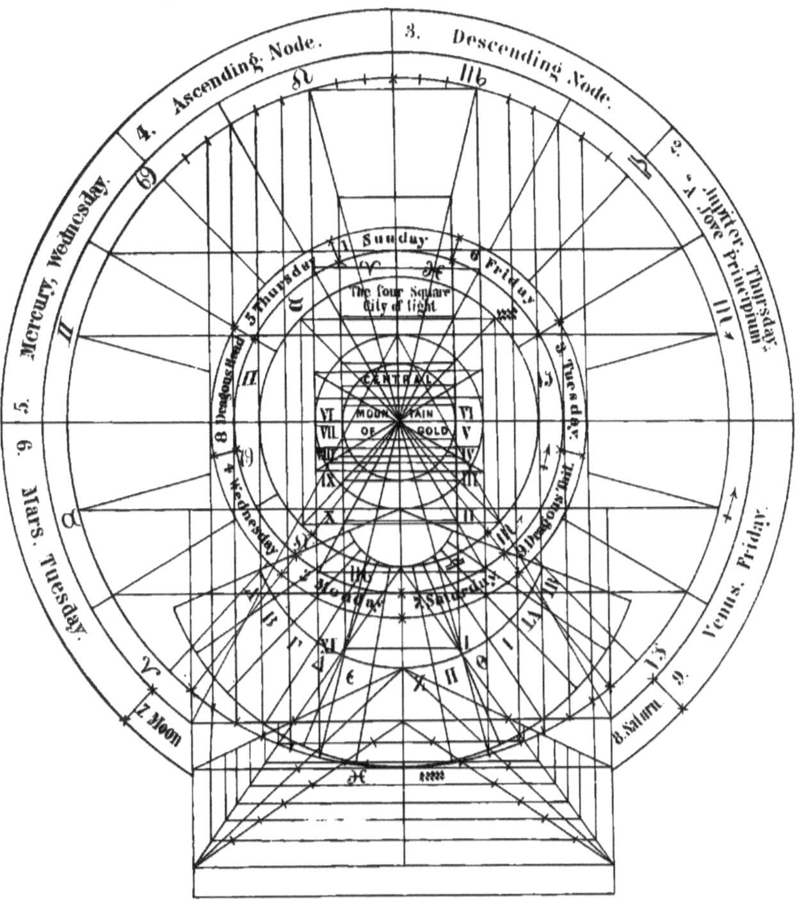

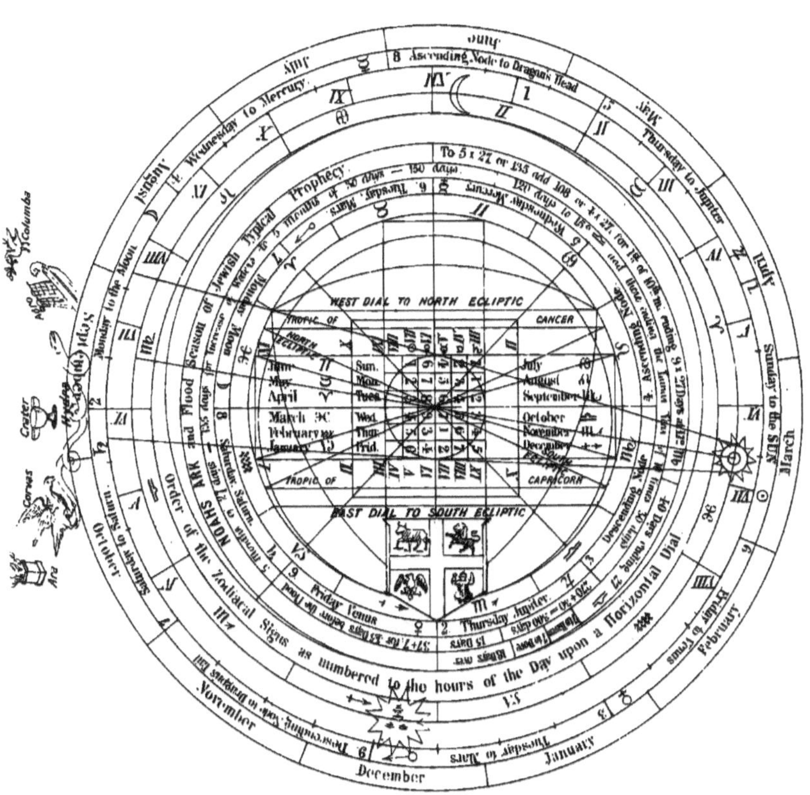
June
8 Ascending Node to Dragon's Head
July
May
Wednesday to Mercury
Thursday to Jupiter
Monday to the Moon
Sunday to the SUN
March
Saturday to Saturn
October
Friday to Venus
February
Tuesday to Mars
January
December
November
9 Descending Node to Dragon's Tail
NOAHS ARK and Flood Season of Jewish Typical Prophecy
To 5 x 27 or 135 add 108 or 4 x 27 for 18 of 108 m. ending 9 x 27 Days at the
WEST DIAL TO NORTH ECLIPTIC
TROPIC OF
CANCER
EAST DIAL TO SOUTH ECLIPTIC
TROPIC OF
CAPRICORN
June
May
April
March
February
January
Sun.
Mon.
Tues.
Wed.
Thur.
Frid.
July
August
September
October
November
December
Saturday. Saturn.
Friday Venus
Thursday Jupiter
Order of the Zodiacal Signs as numbered to the hours of the Day upon a Horizontal Dial
Columba
Crater
Hydra
Corvus
Ara

THE TWO ZODIACS OF THE HINDUS,

Harmonised with the Egyptian Zodiac of Tentyra, Denderah.

It appears thus that their apparent diversities of form followed the differences which occurred from time to time in the ancient dialling of the Orientals.

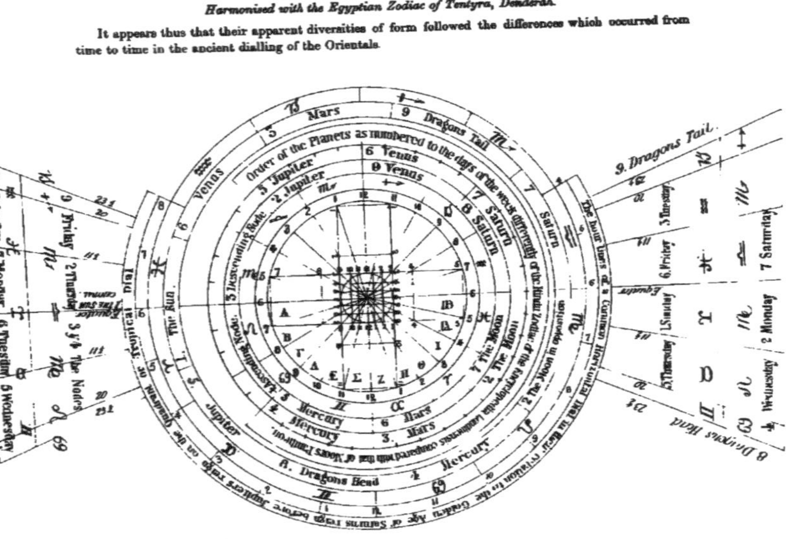

N.B.—The Greek letters mark the relation of the curved part on the Oriental dial with steps (as a mode of dialling for the day of twelve hours, in its relation to that of twice seven hours tropically reckoned) to the Polar Equinoctial, with its parallel hour-lines of 6 × 15 = 90° approximately compared with 7 × 12 = 84°.

For I now seem to have conclusive proof that the hour-lines on the curved part of the Alexandrine Dial were drawn with *Radius* (the *javelin* of Pheron, son of Sesostris, by which, when thrown into the Nile, its waters rose from the 15 cubits of Gen. vi, 20, to the 18 cubits of Herod. ii, c. 111), tangent 18, and its multiples or Tan. 18, 36, 54, and 72, for 15, 30, 45, 60, and 75. Thus when 12 × 18 represented the 216 years numbered to the reign of the 8 *oldest god-kings of the Summer season in Egypt*, 12 × 12° (as 8 × 18 years for the 18 Ethiopians of Herodotus), represented the Winter day of Man's communion with God on earth, as measured by 144°, *for the 144 multiplied thousands over the first-fruits of the world's redemption in Christ, as children of light and of the day. For thus the language of Jewish typical prophecy* divided between the religion of the Jews, compared with that of Egyptian idolatry, as between light and darkness, *under a metaphor derived from the Egyptian dialling of those days, as confirmed by the preternatural darkness from the 6th to the 9th hour at our Lord's crucifixion.*

Thus 7 × 5° = 35°, for two hours of 18° = 36° eastward, and 36° westward on the side steps, form the supplement of 108°, for half the diurnal arc of 12 × 18, compared with half the equinoctial, or 12 × 15 = 180°. Also 2 × 35, or 70 + 105 = 175, or half the lunar cycle of 350, as half Noah's life after the flood.

In the Tropical or Quadrant Dialling of the ancient Orientals the Equinoctial points were placed midway in ♈ and ♎ as by the Egyptians when placing the THOTH of their year midway in ♑. This is the form followed by modern Diallists in the construction of the Trigon, when setting ♑ in the south, on their left hand.

For Enoch's description of the Moon going forth northward with the Sun from his fourth gate (viz., ♎ as fourth from ♑), for two circuits of seven days, or "the bright fortnight of his northern path" between new and full Moon; but turning from the Sun for the two waning circuits of seven days from the place of her opposition, viz., when returning from ♈ to ♎.

For Enoch's description of the Sun and Moon going forth together *southward from* the Sun's *third* eastern gate, *for two lunar circuits of seven days, which preceded the Moon's opposition at full;* as the beginning of her waning course for two other circuits of seven days, until change from the third to second gate for Friday and Saturday.

These lunar circuits of seven days were each measured by an arc of 90°. Hence when the Sun and Moon went forth together southward from ♓ inclusive (as third from ♑), the first circuit would terminate at ♑ for Tuesday, on a comparison of weeks and months. The second circuit of seven days terminated at the place of the Moon's opposition to the Sun in ♓. The third circuit extended over Wednesday, and the fourth over Thursday, to the Sun's third gate again, as the place of the Moon's change from the Sun's third to his second gate, for Friday and Saturday.

The days of the week, with the hours of day and night, as numbered to the planets in Blundevil's 'book of the Sphere,' p. 373; in a form to illustrate the relation of the seven parallel hour-lines on the Steps to the twelve radiating hour-lines on the curved part of the Alexandrine Dial with Steps.

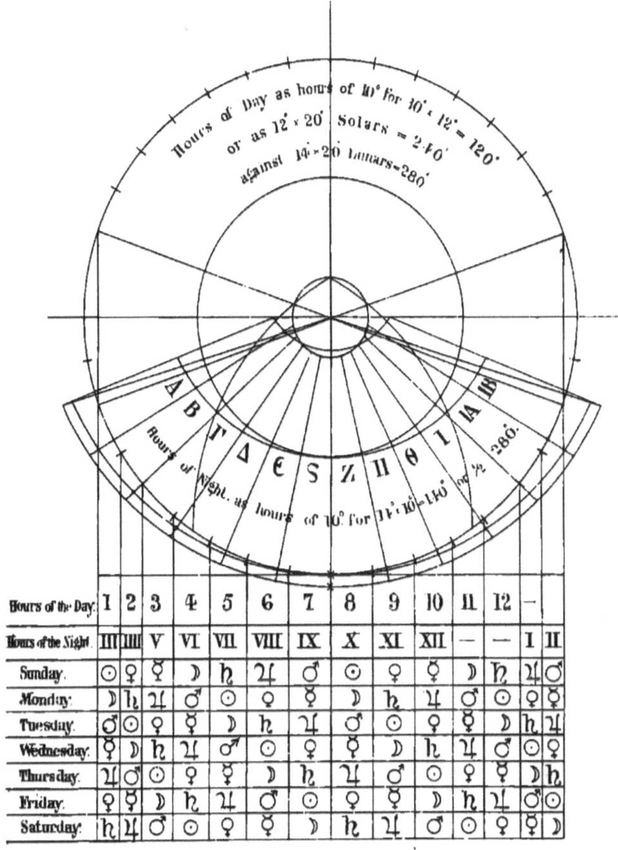

Hours of the Day.	1	2	3	4	5	6	7	8	9	10	11	12	—	
Hours of the Night.	III	IIII	V	VI	VII	VIII	IX	X	XI	XII	—	—	I	II
Sunday.	☉	♀	☿	☽	♄	♃	♂	☉	♀	☿	☽	♄	♃	♂
Monday.	☽	♄	♃	♂	☉	♀	☿	☽	♄	♃	♂	☉	♀	☿
Tuesday.	♂	☉	♀	☿	☽	♄	♃	♂	☉	♀	☿	☽	♄	♃
Wednesday.	☿	☽	♄	♃	♂	☉	♀	☿	☽	♄	♃	♂	☉	♀
Thursday.	♃	♂	☉	♀	☿	☽	♄	♃	♂	☉	♀	☿	☽	♄
Friday.	♀	☿	☽	♄	♃	♂	☉	♀	☿	☽	♄	♃	♂	☉
Saturday.	♄	♃	♂	☉	♀	☿	☽	♄	♃	♂	☉	♀	☿	☽

From the sixth to the ninth hour, on this mode of dialling, meant from twelve at noon to three P.M., or the time of evening prayer.

This, therefore, means from noon for the rest of the day, which is the case with the sun's shadow on the East Dial.

CONSTRUCTION OF A HOLLOW DIAL,

Representing two Sextants of the Equinoctial, for N. lat. 54°; and subtended by Seven Steps, analogous in form to the Egyptian Dial with Steps, brought from Alexandria, and now in the British Museum.

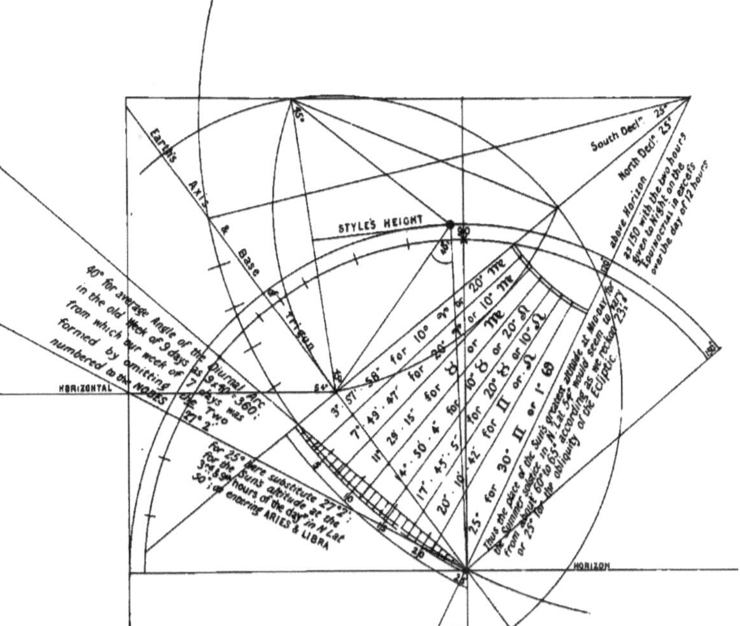

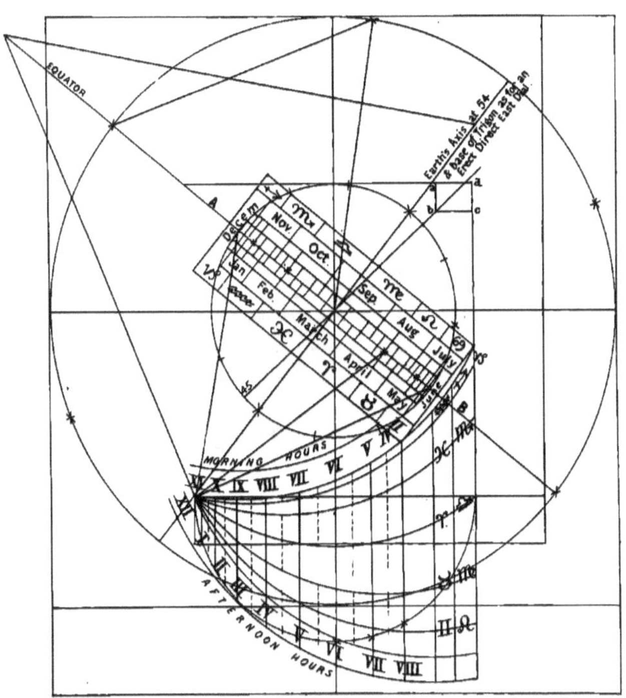

FERGUSON'S KITE-SHAPED PORTABLE DIAL ON CARD;

Combined with an East Side-view of a Dial with Steps for Whitby (say N. Lat. 54°); Modelled after the Greek Egyptian Dial with Steps, brought from Alexandria, and now in the British Museum.

DIRECTIONS FOR USING THE PORTABLE CARD DIAL.

(*From Ferguson's Lectures, p.* 207.)

"The lines *a d*, *a b*, and *b c*, of the Gnomon, must be cut quite through the card; and as the end *a b* of the Gnomon is raised occasionally above the plane of the Dial, it turns upon the uncut line *c d*, as on a hinge.

"The line dotted A B (viz., that dividing between the Eastern and Western Hemispheres on the Analemma, W. II.), must be slit quite through the card, and the thread C. must be put through the slit, and have a knot tied behind to keep it from being easily drawn out. On the other end of this thread is a small plummet D, and on the middle of it a small bead for showing the hour of the day.

"To rectify this Dial, set the thread in the slit right against the day of the month,* and stretch the thread from the day of the month over the angular point where the curve lines meet at XII.; then shift the bead to that point on the thread, and the Dial will be rectified.

"To find the hour of the day, raise the Gnomon, no matter how much or how little (the object being merely to identify the actual shadow with the horizontality of the shadow line, W. II.), and hold the edge of the Dial next the Gnomon towards the sun, so as the uppermost edge of the shadow of the Gnomon may just cover the *shadow line;* and the bead then playing freely on the face of the Dial by the weight of the plummet, will show the time of day among the hour lines, as it is forenoon or afternoon.

"To find the time of sun-rising and setting, move the thread amongst the hour lines until it covers some one of them, or lies parallel betwixt any two, and then it will cut the time of sun-rising among the forenoon hours, and of sun-setting among the afternoon hours, for that day of the year to which the thread is set in the scale of months.

"To find the sun's declination, stretch the thread from the day of the month over the angular point at XII., and it will cut the sun's declination, as it is north or south, for that day in the proper scale.

"To find on what days the sun enters the signs, when the bead, as above rectified, moves along any of the curve lines which have the signs of the zodiac marked upom them, the sun enters those signs on the days pointed out by the thread in the scale of the months."

---

* This can only be done approximately on a small scale. The divisions of 10 days are reduced to those of 5 by the dots between the linear divisions of 3 times 10 for each month. The rest must be done ideally.

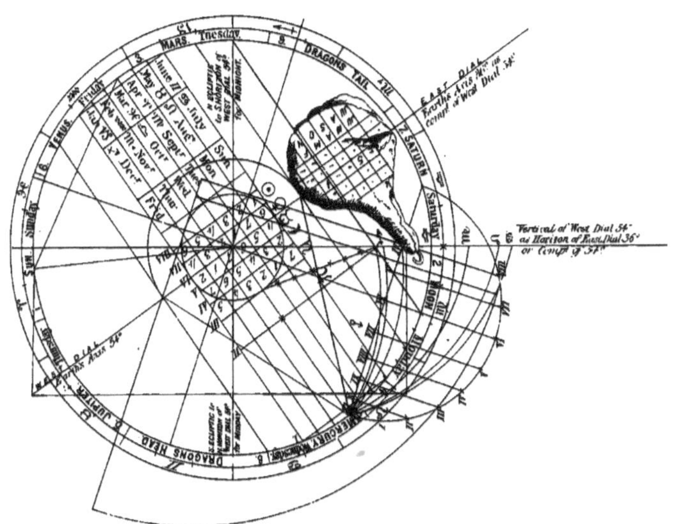

The Horological Value of the Parallel Lines on the Steps of the Greek-Egyptian Dial, found at Alexandria, were ascertained to demonstration, by comparison with the Upper Inclined East Dialling of Bedos de Celles, also with the Portable Meridian and Calendarium of the Ham Dial.

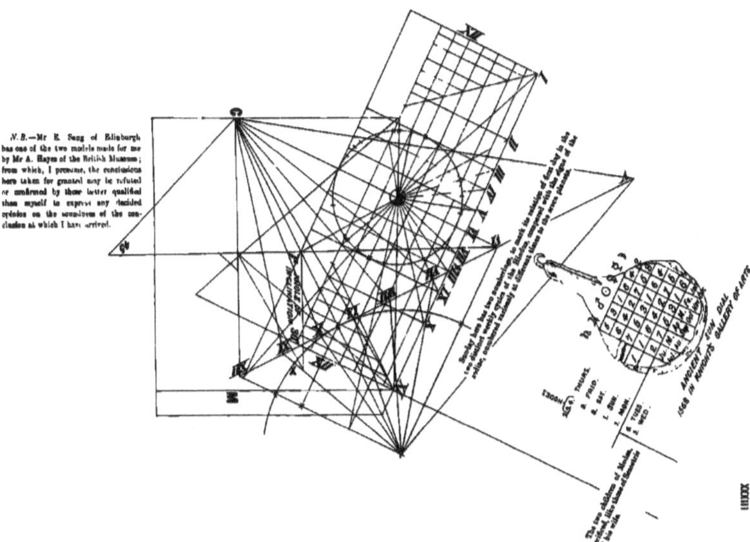

N.B.—Mr E. Sang of Edinburgh has one of the two models made for me by Mr A. Hayes of the British Museum; from which, I presume, the conclusions here taken for granted may be refuted or confirmed by those better qualified than myself to express any decided opinion on the soundness of the conclusion at which I have arrived.

THE STRUCTURE OF THE ALEXANDRINE OR GREEK EGYPTIAN DIAL, WITH STEPS, RECONSIDERED GNOMONICALLY, ALSO THAT OF ANOTHER VERY CURIOUS SUN-DIAL IN THE SHAPE OF A HAM.

The **Ham-Dial** seemingly has a Calendar thereon. The 30 (or 5 × 6) divisions seem to number six cycles of 5 days to each lunation of 30 days. But whether numerals or not, the markings are illegible. Three, however, may be identified, on the supposition of its being a West Dial with Earth's axis on the hour-line of Six; for the equinoctial points must be brought under the brass meridian and the solstitial points given to the east and west horizon of the Celestial Globe; for a reckoning of the diurnal arc as beginning at XII. o'clock, whether mid-night or mid-day. But the calendaring will hold good for an East *and* West, or Polar Equinoctial Dial, with Earth's axis on the hour-line of XII., as represented below.

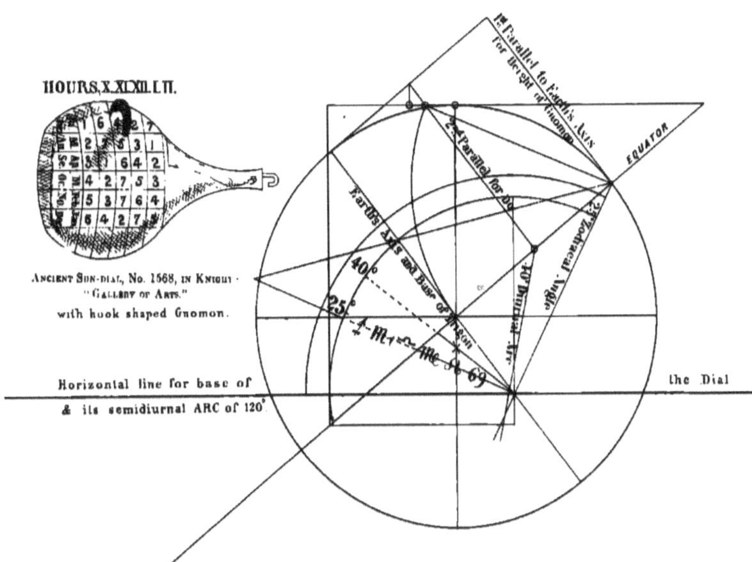

ANCIENT SUN-DIAL, No. 1568, IN KNIGHT'S "GALLERY OF ARTS." with hook shaped Gnomon.

* Compare the beginning of the diurnal arc from VIRGO, with the words of Ovid: "Jam redit et VIRGO, redeunt SATURNIA regna." Also the starting of the Argonauts *at evening*, when sailing from West to East to bring back *the golden fleece;* associating, as the ancients did, each renewal of the diurnal arc with the sunset of the previous day. Note also, in the week of 9 days each diurnal arc was measured by 40 degrees on the circle. This was associated with the division of years and lunations into 3 parts only, an arrangement preserved by the idolators after the re-institution of the Sabbatic ordinance by Moses; for under that, years and lunations were thenceforth to be typically divided into 4 parts,—substituting 4 × 7 = 28, for 3 × 9 = 27, or 3 × 10 = 30,—*to perpetuate a typical memorial of the primeval Sabbath.* When the 8 gods reigned in Egypt ((for the *weekly* and *monthly* cycle of 8 was *idolatrously* substituted by Jeroboam, Kings xii. 32, for the Jewish Feast of Tabernacles in the *seventh* month), the diurnal arc measured 45°; for 8 × 45 = 360. In this cycle no account was taken of *Sunday;* but in *Noah's week* of 9 days, out of which the week of 7 days arose (by omitting the 2 numbered to the NODES of ascending and descending light) *Sunday* characterised *the first day* of the week, or day following the Sabbath; as under the typical dispensation of Moses to the Jews in redemption from bondage, to the idolatrous worship of the Egyptians, Sunday marked the beginning, and the Sabbath the close, of typical time. Hence the relation of the Seventh Seal, the Seventh Trumpet, and the Seventh Vial (in the Apocalyptic Vision) to the close of the Mosaic or typical dispensation; assimilated to the ingathering of the vintage, at the close of the Jewish harvest season, with the seventh month of their typical time

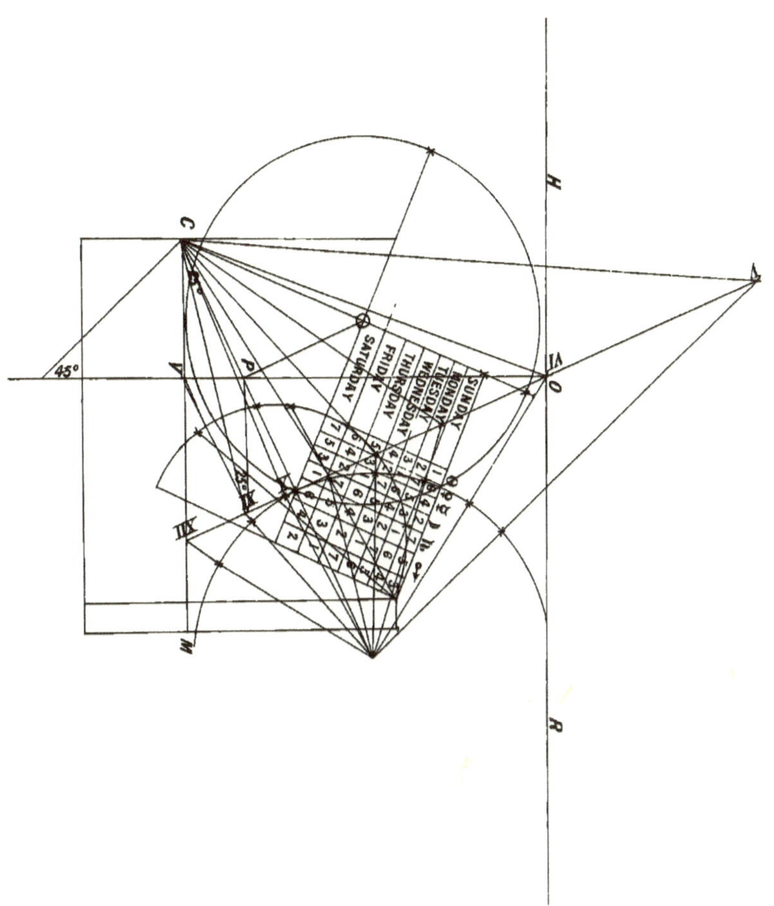
SUNDAY
MONDAY
TUESDAY
WEDNESDAY
THURSDAY
FRIDAY
SATURDAY
H
C
VI
O
P
A
45°
XII
M
R

The Typical Structure of the Greek-Egyptain Dial with Steps, self-explained upon a front view, so as to mark the relation of the lowest curve to the Equinoctial.

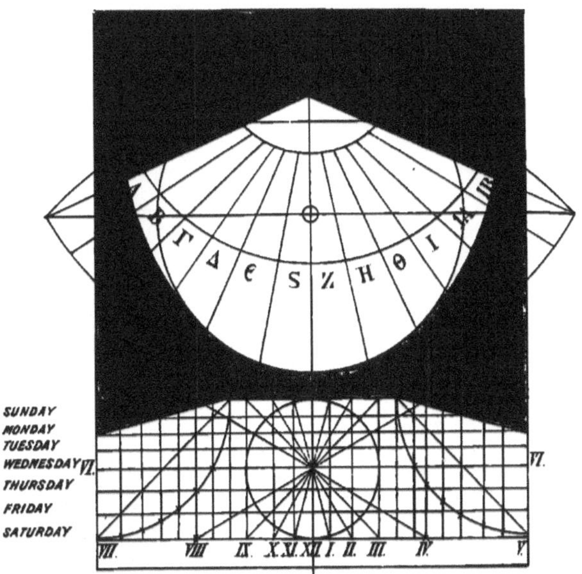

The centre from which to draw the uppermost curve of this Dial is the centre of the little circle on the Steps.

Front view of a Dial with Steps for N. lat. 54°, from a model made after the Greek-Egyptian Dial with Steps, brought from Alexandria, and now in the British Museum.

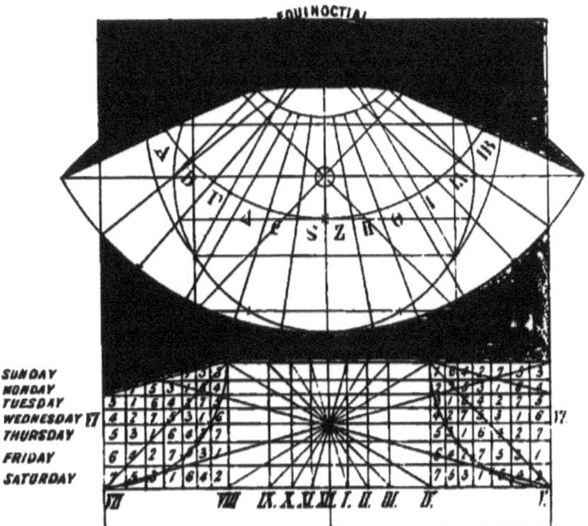

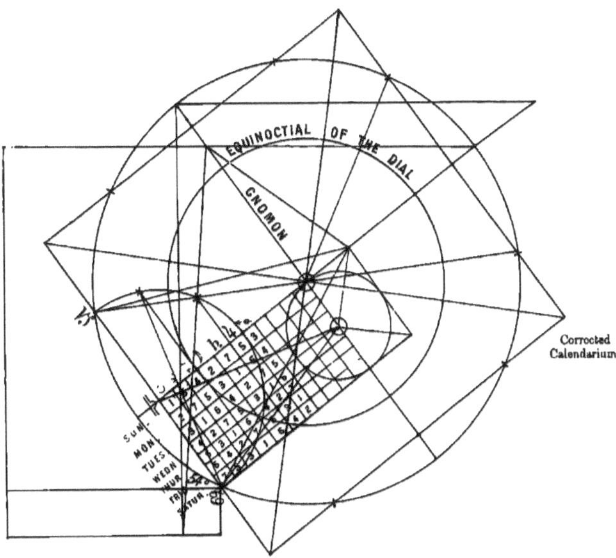

West face of the Alexandrine Dial with Steps; as, seemingly, the face to which the Calendarium on the Steps applies.

Compare this Calendarium (as given thus to the Sun's north declination) with the statue of 25 cubits high, which Rhampsinitus erected to Summer, at the west entrance of the Temple of Vulcan. He also erected another of the same dimensions, and in the same place, to Winter.

But Divine offerings were made only to that of Summer, that of Winter being held in no honour at all.

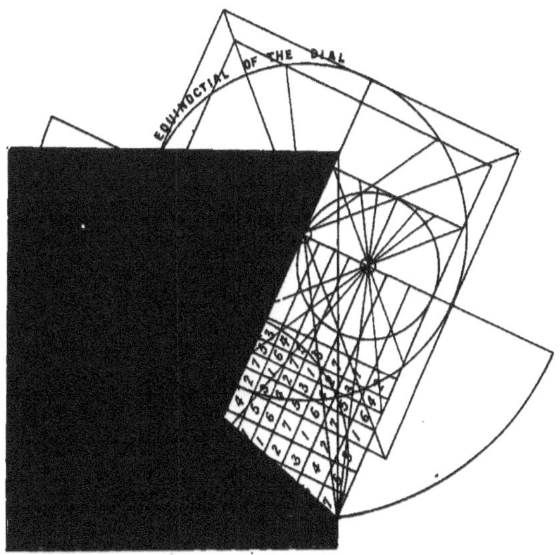

West face of a Dial with Steps for N. lat. 54, from a model of the Alexandrine, or Greek-Egyptian Dial with Steps; the typical object and structure of which are here assumed to be now clearly ascertained.

Law of the steps subtending the curved part of the Alexandrine or Greek-Egyptian Dial, with steps, as adapting to the *Tetarton* (or East and West Dialling of the Egyptians) the semicircular dialling of the Chaldæans, which Berosus invented *by hollowing it out of a square, and inclining it to the latitude*. The square was seemingly formed on a chord of 120°, *for a circular analogy between the year of three seasons and the year of four seasons.*

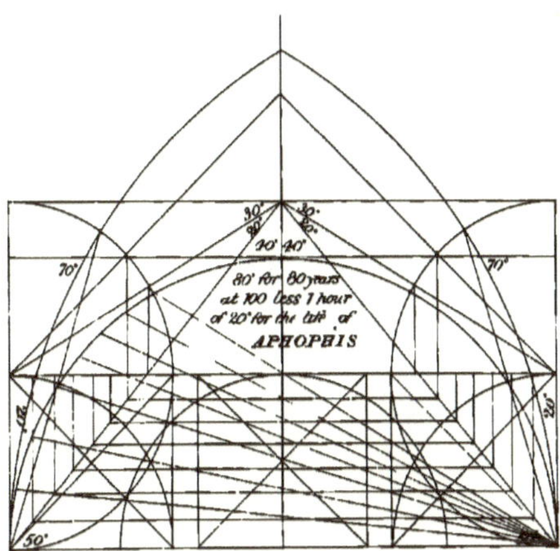

This is clearly capable of a variable adaptation from the 6 × 10 = 60 on the side steps (2 Kings xx, 8–12) to 7 × 8 + 4 = 60 ; 7 × 9 = 63 ; 7 × 10 = 70 ; 7 × 12 = 84 ; and 7 × 15 = 105, for N. Lat. 30°.

It appears, from the above analysis of the construction, that the front steps divided the quadrant of 90°, on the line of sines, into 6 times 10°, leaving 30° to the top step.

It also raises a presumption that the three small pyramids between the same parallel lines, and close together at Ghizeh, as above, did represent the same typical design as the steps of this dial.

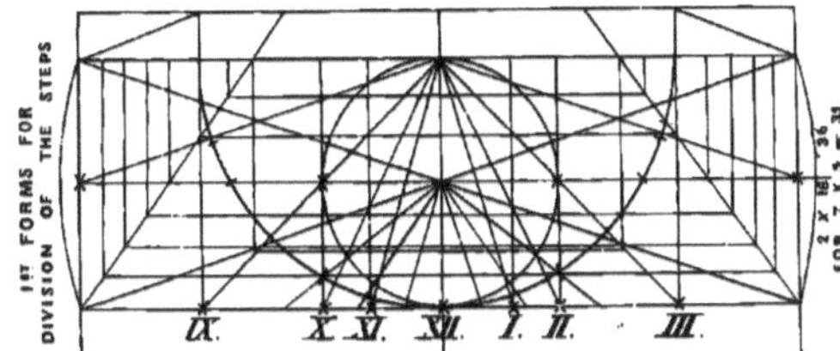

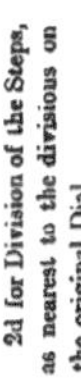

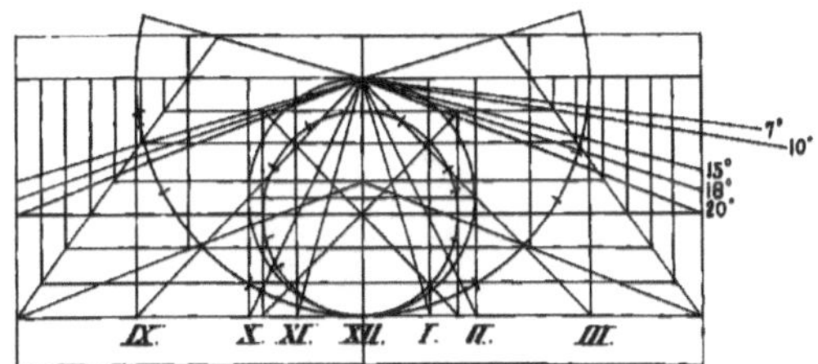

This puts out 7° from the Equinoctial, on both sides, for the top steps, leaving the Quadrant of 90, reduced to the 83 years' reign of Helius, for 7 × 12 = 84, compared with 6 × 15 = 90.

N.B.—180, less 2 × 20 or 40, give 140, for the semi-lunar arc of 280, to the front of the Dial.

The Steps of the Alexandrine or Greek-Egyptian Dial, measured in their relation to the *semi equinoctial* of the Dial, by way of tracing more exactly the typical and horological value of the Symbolism.

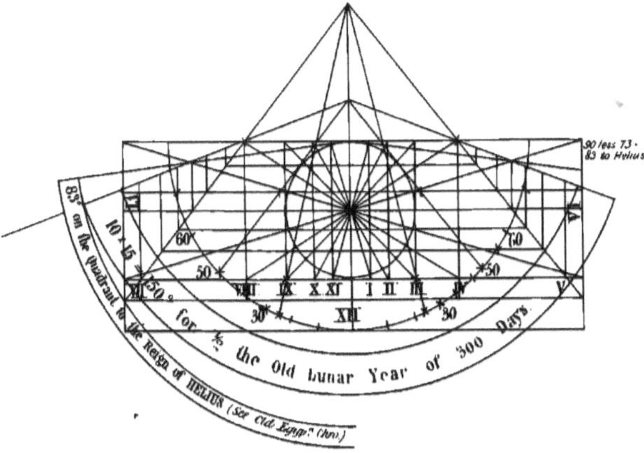

The Steps, for a Dial with Steps in N. lat. 54°, imitating that of Greek-Egyptian construction brought from Alexandria, and now in the British Museum.

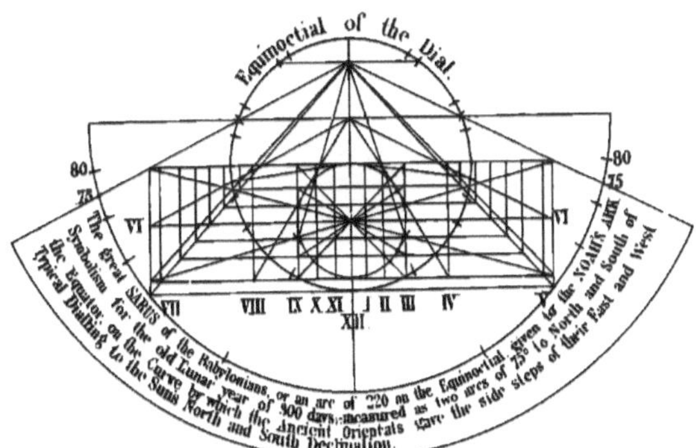

Relation of the Steps to the Equinoctial, for a Dialling with Steps in N. Lat. 54°, like that of the Ancient Orientals.

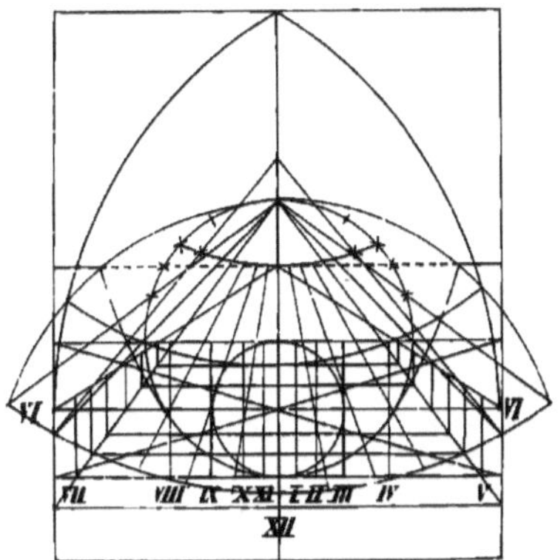

Imitation of the Egyptian Dial with Steps, for N. lat. 54°—from a model tried in the Sun, with a satisfactory result—for numbering seven planetary hours of Enoch (viz. 7 × 20° = 10 × 14° or 140°) to the day of ten hours, on a Polar Equinoctial Dial. (Compare the top of this symbolism with the canopy to the shrine for Subhadra, between Juggarnath and Bala Rama.)

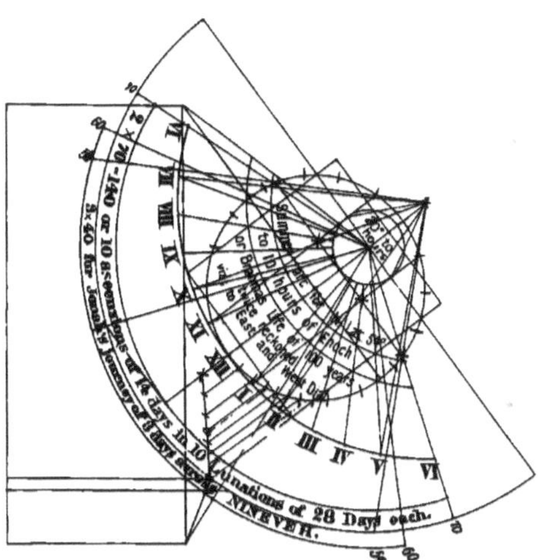

Cutting off 40° from the Equinoctial—by the four-square symbolism—for the 100 years' life of Brahmah, we have, northward and southward, the Divine age of 10 times 5 degrees of the Equinoctial read as 7 times 7 on the steps, and reckoned as days, for a harmony between the Jewish feast of weeks and the Divine age in the typical chronology of their heathen neighbours.

Similarly, the steps might be made to compare 10 weeks of 7 days with 7 weeks of ten days. The former of these was Enoch's celebrated span of typical and prophetic time.

The Hindu Zodiac for the week of nine days, as 9 × 40 = 360, on the Equinoctial, reduced (by the symbolism for the four-square City of Light, or the new Jerusalem within the Equinoctial) to nine hours of Enoch, as hours of 20°, or 80 minutes to an hour. These represent the diurnal half of the Equinoctial, as given to the 18 Ethiopians of Herodotus, for 18 × 20° = 360°.

This typical Dialling gave *the Western Horizon* to North lat. for an astronomical reckoning of the day from noon to midnight, on an erect direct West Dial in North lat. It seems to be, in this sense, that the primeval day of Jewish tradition was said to have begun "*at evening time*," viz., as the Sun was turning from East to West. (*See* Zech. xiv. 7, and Gen. i. 14.) This symbolism answers to that in Ezekiel's prophetic vision of heaven as God's throne (chap. i. 10); for it places the zodiacal sign "*Leo*" *to the right of the meridian*, whereas the idolatrous worshippers of the rising sun, on an erect direct East Dial, would place "*Taurus*" on the right of the meridian. Hence, I suspect, that the ignorance of the Ninevites, in not being able to discern between their right hand and their left, Jonah iv. 11, had respect to an idolatrous deviation from the Jewish typical symbolism, which would place "*Leo*" *on the right of the meridian, in its Dialling notice of typical and prophetic time.* This, moreover, explains the meaning of Ezek. viii. 16, as referring to 25 idolatrous worshippers of the rising sun, within the typical sanctuary of Mosaic ordinance. For that placed the Holy of Holies at the west end, and the altar to the north-east of the porch. The worshippers of the rising sun, from an altar thus situated, must of necessity, in turning their faces to the East, have stood with their backs towards the most holy place, *instead of worshipping towards it, as required by their typical law.* The 25 idolators seem numbered to the 25° of the then zodiacal angle.

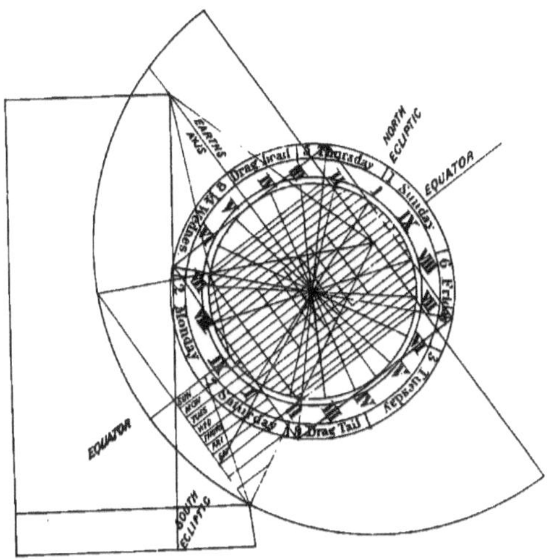

XLVI

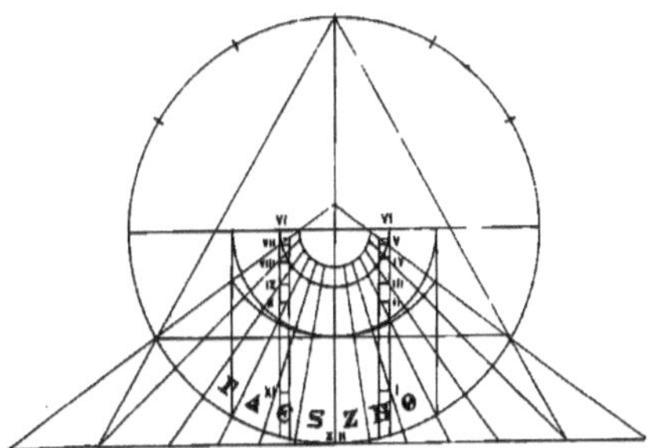

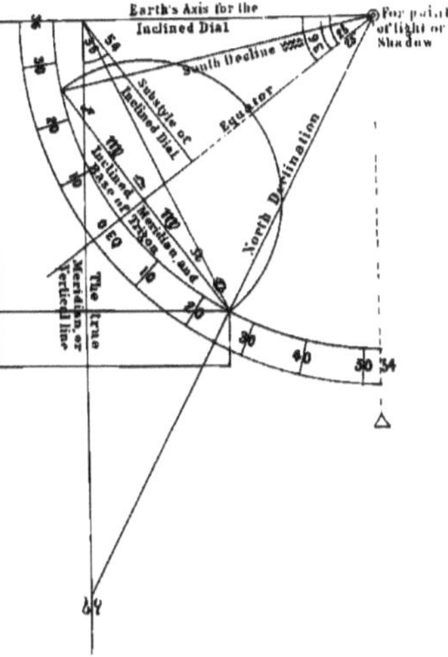

West Side of a Dial for N. Lat. 54°, constructed like the Greek-Egyptian Dial with Steps.

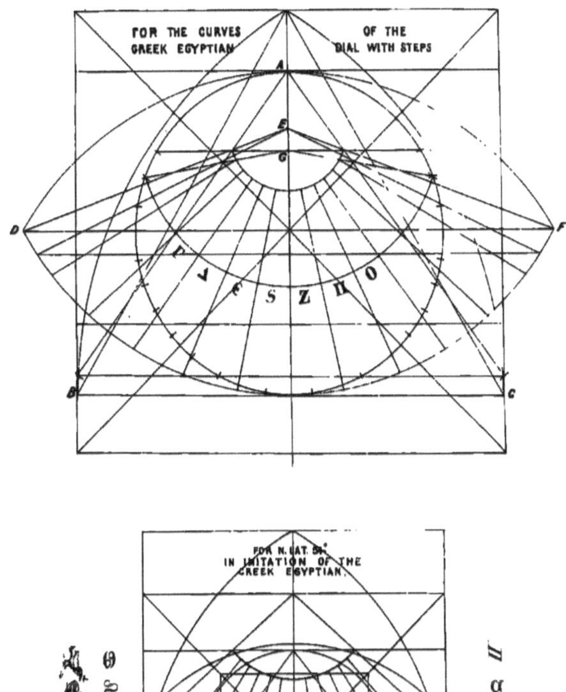

FOR N. LAT. 51°
IN IMITATION OF THE
GREEK EGYPTIAN.

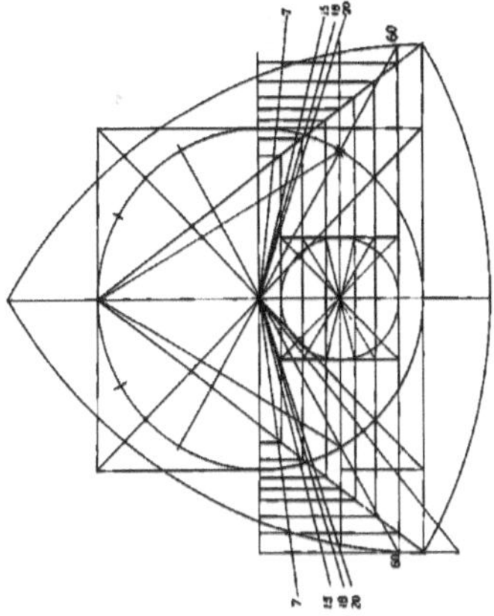

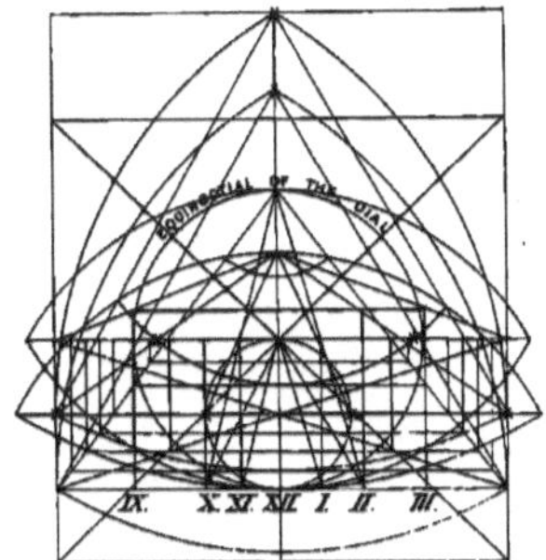

Relation of the Steps to the Equinoctial for a Dialling with Steps in N. Lat. 54°, like that of the Ancient Greek-Egyptian for N. Lat. 30°.

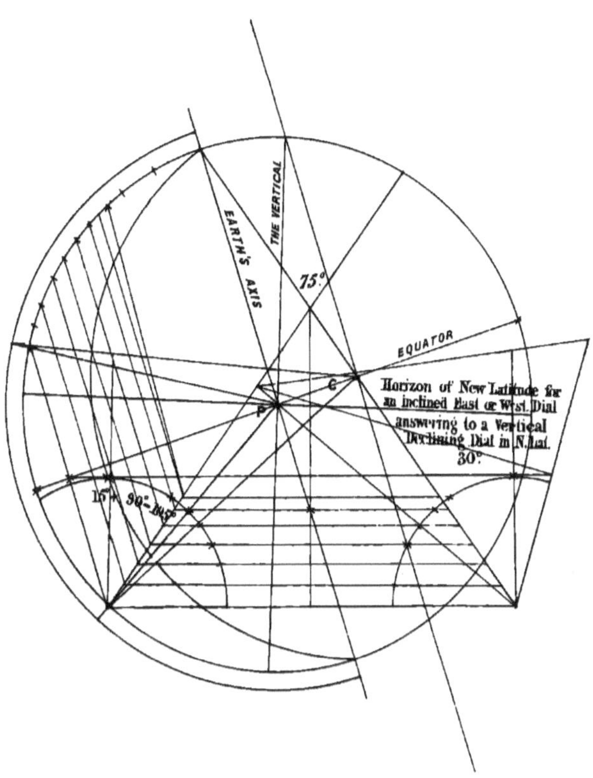
THE VERTICAL
EARTH'S AXIS
75°
EQUATOR
C
P
Horizon of New Latitude for an inclined East or West Dial answering to a Vertical Declining Dial in N. Lat. 30°.
15°
90°-105°

An Upper East Dial *inclined* at 50°, with elevation of the Pole at 25°, as a declining vertical for lat. 65°, with a declination of 50°, to illustrate the structure of the Alexandrine Dial by imitating that of Bedos de Celes, inclined at 47° 15′, with elevation of the Pole at 48°.

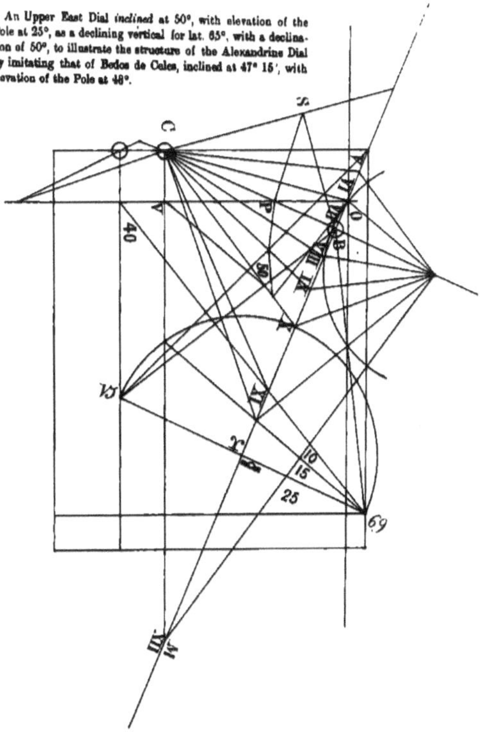

An upper-inclined East Dial for N. lat. 65, with inclination of 45°, constructed after the rule of Bedos de Celes, for an explanation of the Alexandrine Dial, on the supposition of its not being a South Vertical, but an East and West Dial.

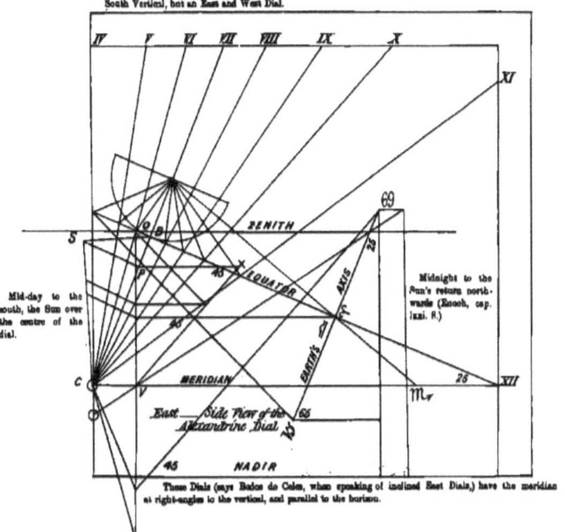

These Dials (says Bedos de Celes, when speaking of inclined East Dials,) have the meridian at right-angles to the vertical, and parallel to the horizon.

Harmony of the Egyptian and Hindu Zodiacs in their relation to the structure and object of the Greek-Egyptian Dial with steps; or their Dialling of the Ptolemaic era, as a combination of their South vertical with the East and West Dialling. This was probably derived from the Dial of Ahaz, as a Dial with steps.

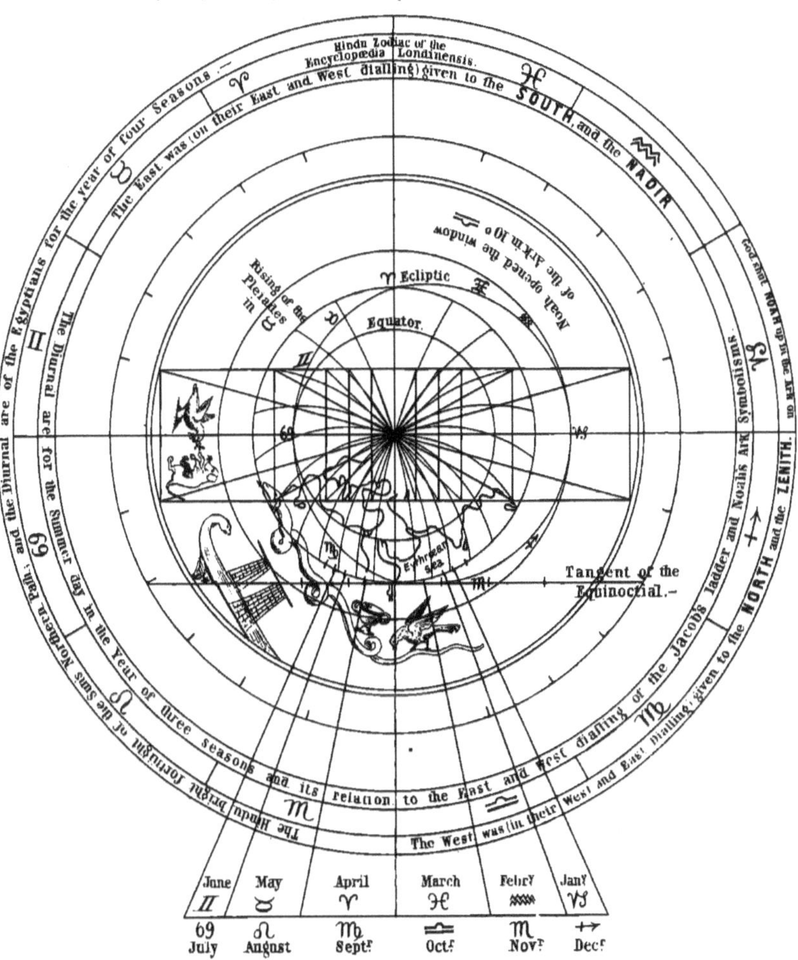

N.B.—To 180° – 210° add 30° (*for the hour going out on the East and West Dial of the Orientals, and therefore to be reckoned as two hours on their Equinoctial Dial*), and we have the year of eleven months, or 330 days, converted into the old Chaldean Solar year of 360 days.

The MYSTICA VANNUS BACCHI,

or Mystic Fan of Bacchus—proving the symbolic connection which exists between the structure of the ancient Greek-Egyptian Dial, with steps, and the astronomical design of the Great Pyramid, as explained by Professor C. PIAZZI SMYTH, Astronomer Royal for Scotland.

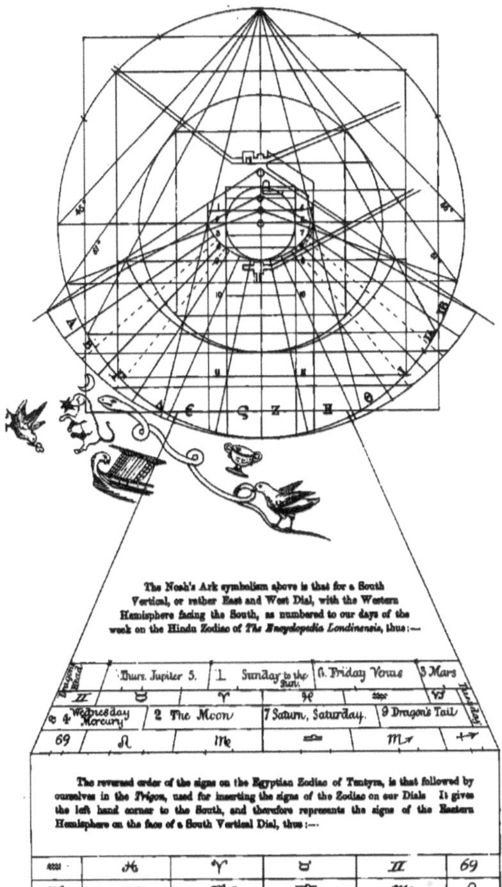

The Noah's Ark symbolism above is that for a South Vertical, or rather East and West Dial, with the Western Hemisphere facing the South, as numbered to our days of the week on the Hindu Zodiac of *The Encyclopedia Londinensis*, thus:—

Dragon's Head	Thurs. Jupiter 5.	1 Sunday to the Sun.		6. Friday Venus	3 Mars
♊	♉	♈	♓	♒	♑
☋ 4 Wednesday Mercury	2 The Moon	7 Saturn, Saturday.		9 Dragon's Tail	Tuesday
♋	♌	♍	♎	♏	♐

The reversed order of the signs on the Egyptian Zodiac of Tentyra, is that followed by ourselves in the *Trigon*, used for inserting the signs of the Zodiac on our Dials. It gives the left hand corner to the South, and therefore represents the signs of the Eastern Hemisphere on the face of a South Vertical Dial, thus:—

♒	♓	♈	♉	♊	♋
♑	♐	♏	♎	♍	♌

The Ecliptic in this form is spanned by the image of Osiris, as that of the colossal image of four metals seen by Nebuchadnezzar in his dream, on the Egyptian Zodiac of Tentyra.

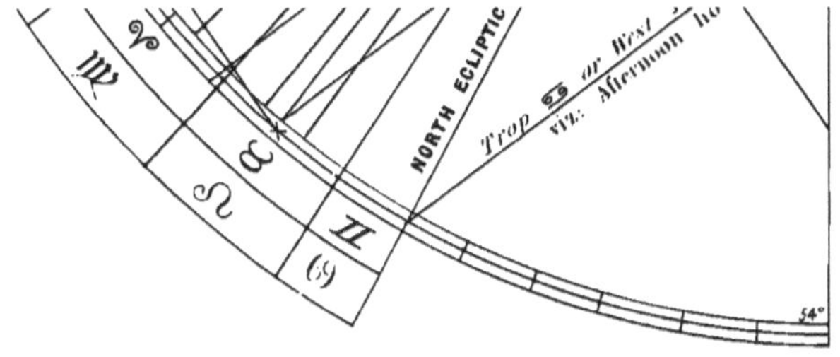

An East & West Quadrant Dial, for N. Lat. 54°

* The XII.th hour, or the meridian, and plane of the prime vertical, taken for the HORIZON, or dividing line between east and west longitude; as the Ancient Egyptians divided their country to the east and west by the Nile, and as the Jews similarly divided the Holy Land by the Jordan.

Compare the Egyptian tradition, that Rhampsinitus erected at the West Entrancé of the Temple of Vulcan two statues of twenty-five cubits in height,—the one to Summer and the other to Winter,—with the quadrant stature of the Mithras d'Aries, for the semi-diurnal arc between morning and noon, or from noon to sunset.

An East and West Quadrant Dial for N. Lat. 54°, compared with the Structure of the Alexandrine Dial, and with the Calendarium of the Hindu Zodiac for the week of 9 days. This was reduced to 7 (substituting 4 × 7 for 3 × 9 days monthly) by omitting the two numbered to the Nodes and symbolised to the Dragon which encircles MITHRAS; viz., the ascending Node to the Dragon's Head, and the descending Node to the Dragon's Tail; the symbolic Dragon being Hydra, rising in Leo, on the celestial globe. Hence the symbolic Mithras has a lion's head. Thus, on the shield of Hercules, Hesiod (v. 160), tells us there were 12 dragons' heads for 12 successions of lunar light in the year of 12 months.

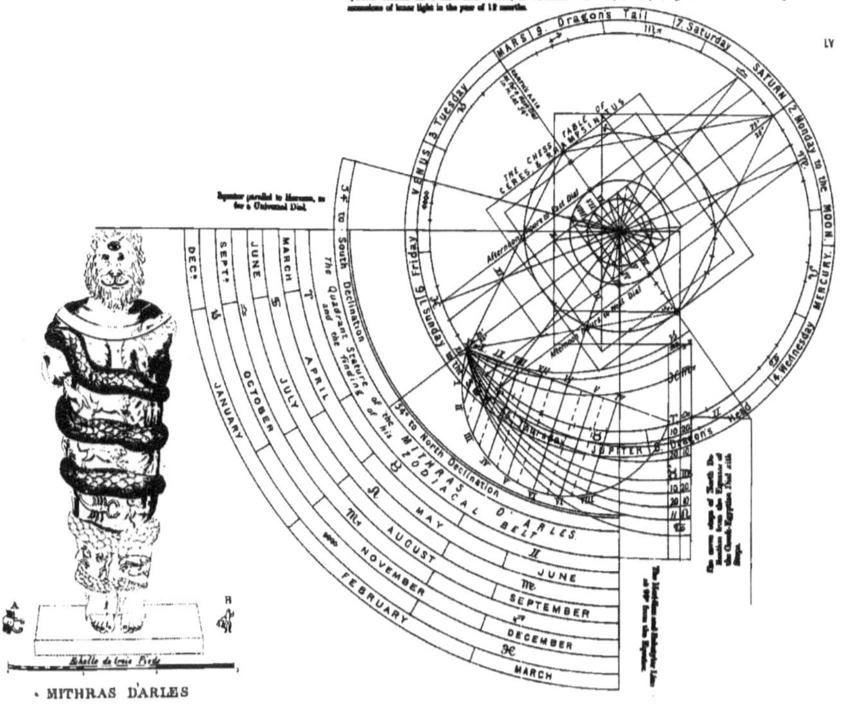

MITHRAS D'ARLES

This Diagram differs from all others on the same subject, by taking for the centre of the outermost circle the east and west hornings of the Dial (in their relation to the base of the trigon for the side steps), instead of the supposed relation of the Equinoctial to another form of central Gnomon, as implied in the models which substitute an inclined for a horizontal top.

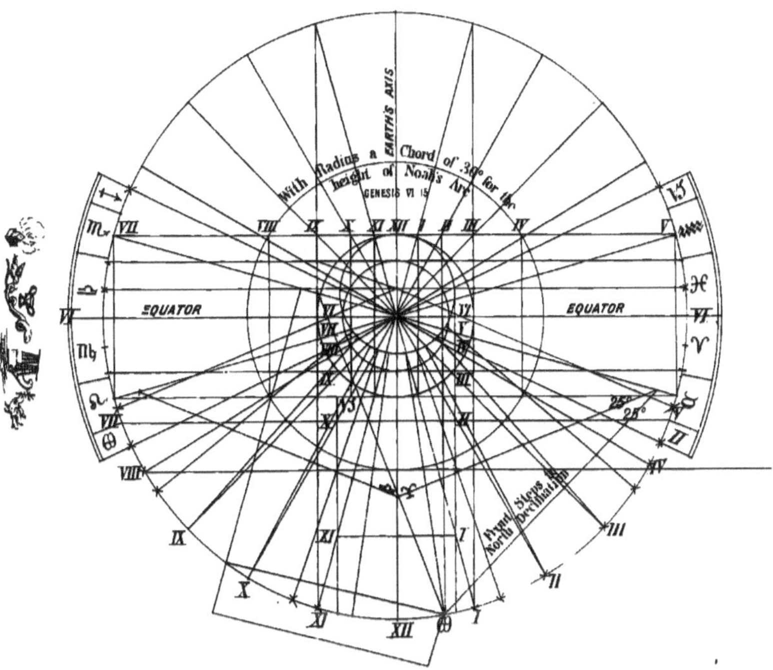

Equinoctial hours compared with those of Blackie's Portable Meridian, on the scale of my last constructed Dial for N. Lat. 54°, in imitation of the Greek-Egyptian Dial with Steps.

The law of the relation between the hours of the Equinoctial and of *the inclined meridian on a Polar Dial with Steps*, seems to be 10 hours of 15° to an hour (for half the old lunar year of 300 days, as that of the Noah's Ark Symbolism, for the year of three seasons), compared with 14 hours of 10° to an hour (or half the old lunar year of 280, as that of the Sabbatarians). Thus the ancient Orientals, in their typical dialling with steps, seem to have divided the angle of 25°, as given by them to the Sun's north declination, as we do that of 23½° to the quadrant of 90°, twice numbered over the diurnal arc, as over the summer half of the year in our north latitude.

The parallel lines on the front steps sub divide this semi-equinoctial of 180 into twice 7 × 10 = 70; leaving out twice 20, for the 40 given to the Culminating Sun for Sunday, instead of 60 to OSIRIS by the idolators.

ALL THE TYPICAL TIMES OF ANCIENT JEWISH PROPHECY NUMBERED UPON A WEST DIAL FOR N. LAT. 25°, COMPARED WITH THE STRUCTURE OF THE GREEK EGYPTIAN DIAL WITH STEPS, BROUGHT FROM ALEXANDRIA AND NOW IN THE BRITISH MUSEUM.

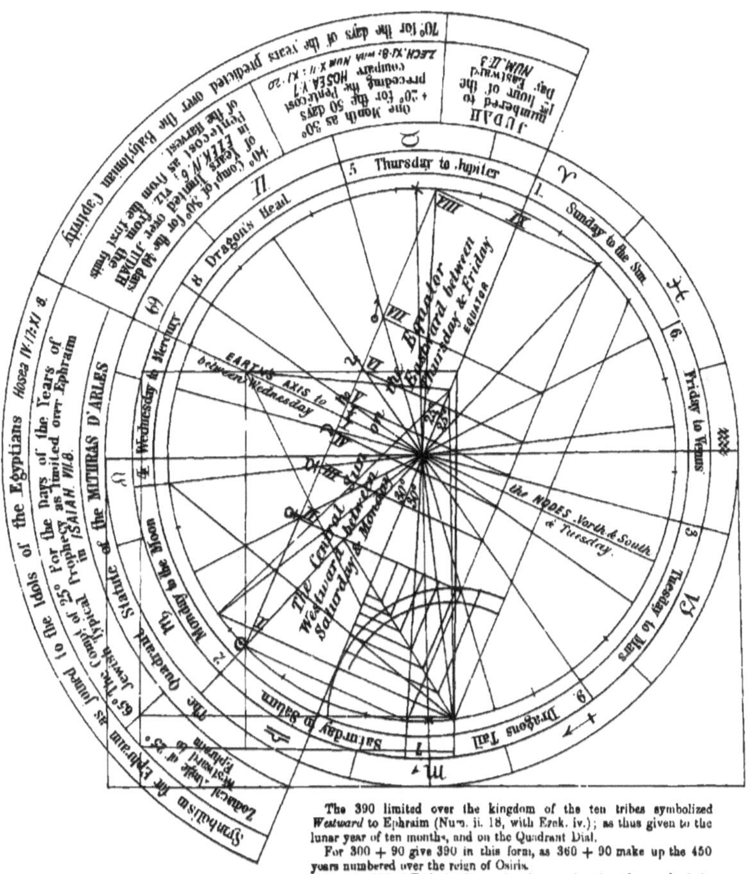

The 390 limited over the kingdom of the ten tribes symbolized *Westward* to Ephraim (Num. ii. 18, with Ezek. iv.); as thus given to the lunar year of ten months, and on the Quadrant Dial.

For 300 + 90 give 390 in this form, as 360 + 90 make up the 450 years numbered over the reign of Osiris.

But the 390 of Ezek. iv. 5, may be also numbered as *the month* of the predicted cutting off, with anniversary reference. Thus 360 + 30 = 390.

The lunar year of 10 × 27 = 9 × 30 is here numbered on the West Dial, as the week of nine days reduced to one of seven, numbered to the seven planetary hours as hours of 20°, or 80 minutes, viz., as the hours of Enoch. For 3½ of 20° = 70, and 2 × 70 = 140, or ½ the lunar year of 280 days. The 2300 of Dan. viii. 14 represent six years, four months, twenty days, or six anniversaries of the winter season, *to one season of seven typical months* in the Sabbath of seven years, for confirming the covenant with many. Thus, 2520 = 2 × 1260 days, or six years, four months, twenty days + seven months, ten days.

THE ECCLESIASTICAL YEAR OF CHRISTIANS, IN ITS RELATION TO THE PRE-EXISTING DIVISIONS OF TIME INTO DAYS OF SACRED AND SECULAR ACCOUNT, BY BOTH JEWS AND HEATHEN.

Calendarium for the weekly cycle of *seven* days in which Saturn reigned, compared with the cycle of Jupiter, or the weekly cycle of five days. By the reigns of Saturn and Jupiter, in their respective cycles, we are to understand that the *seventh* day of the week was dedicated to Saturn, when the *fifth* was dedicated to Jupiter. Thus five Sabbatarian cycles of 70 were as seven of 50, when comparing the postdiluvian lunar year of 350 with the six cycles of OSIRIS, or 6 × 60 numbered to the old Chaldean solar year of 360 days.

The weeks of the ecclesiastical year, as numbered in some of the collects in our Book of Common Prayer, give evidence of their Roman origin; for the ancient Roman missals once numbered six collects to *the month* of Advent,—a season probably limited to one month, with typical reference to *the month* of Zech. xi. 8, and Hosea v. 7.

In the old Roman week of nine days, the Wednesdays and Fridays were days of religious account, and once had separate collects, epistles, and gospels for the month of Advent. (*See* Shepherd, on the Book of Common Prayer, vol. ii., p. 36.)

The names of Septuagesima, Sexagesima, Quinquagesima, and Quadragesima Sundays, show that the collects for those days were framed at a time when the 70 days between Septuagesima and Easter Sunday were thus limited to number ten weeks of seven days, as seven of ten days.

The triangular symbol of the Trinity, within the four-square City of Light (having the hour circle with its radiating hour-lines for their common centre) serves to explain what the Hindus meant by their central mountain of gold, on the zodiac for the week of 9 × 40° = 360°.

From the comparison of the two Hindu zodiacs here made, it is clear that the ancient Orientals numbered the morning hours on their East Dial to the Sun, as *then descending eastward from north to south.* (*See* Enoch, cap. lxxi. v. 8.)

The afternoon hours they numbered on their West Dial, for light ascending from south to north, *westward to the God who gave it.*

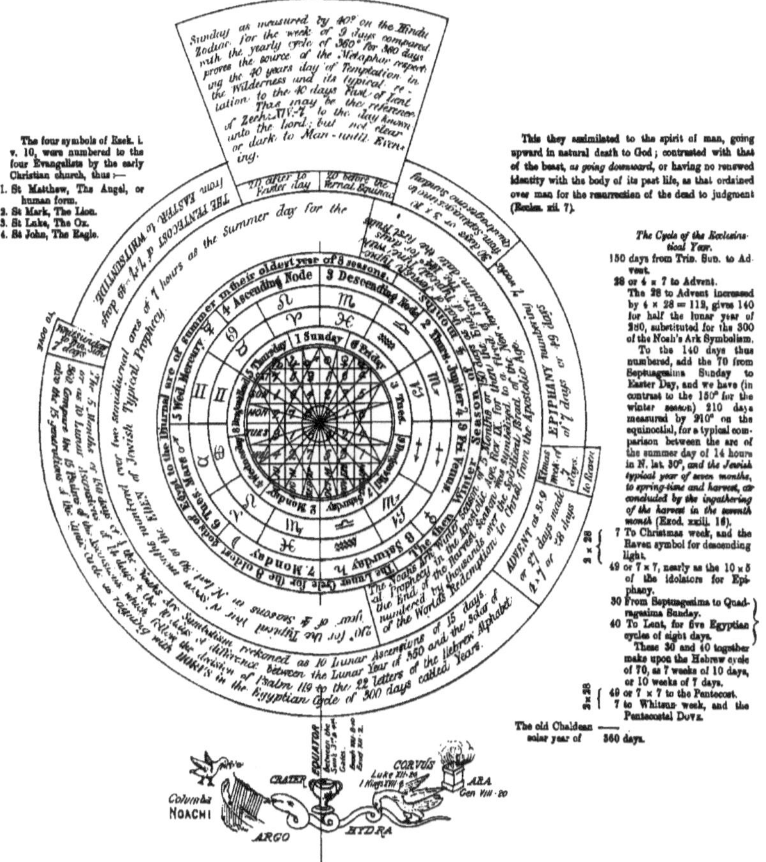

The four symbols of Ezek. i. v. 10, were numbered to the four Evangelists by the early Christian church, thus:—
1. St Matthew, The Angel, or human form.
2. St Mark, The Lion.
3. St Luke, The Ox.
4. St John, The Eagle.

This they assimilated to the spirit of man, going upward in natural death to God; contrasted with that of the beast, *as going downward*, or having no renewed identity with the body of its past life, as that ordained over man for the resurrection of the dead to judgment (Eccles. xii. 7).

The Cycle of the Ecclesiastical Year.

150 days from Trin. Sun. to Advent.

28 or 4 × 7 to Advent.

The 28 to Advent increased by 4 × 28 = 112, gives 140 for half the lunar year of 280, substituted for the 300 of the Noah's Ark Symbolism.

To the 140 days thus numbered, add the 70 from Septuagesima Sunday to Easter Day, and we have (in contrast to the 150° for the winter season) 210 days measured by 210° on the equinoctial, for a typical comparison between the arc of the summer day of 14 hours in N. lat. 30°, *and the Jewish typical year of seven months, to spring-time and harvest, as concluded by the ingathering of the harvest in the seventh month* (Exod. xxiii. 16).

3 × 28 { 7 To Christmas week, and the Raven symbol for descending light.

49 or 7 × 7, nearly as the 10 × 5 of the idolators for Epiphany.

30 From Septuagesima to Quadragesima Sunday.

40 To Lent, for five Egyptian cycles of eight days.

These 30 and 40 together make upon the Hebrew cycle of 70, as 7 weeks of 10 days, or 10 weeks of 7 days.

2 × 28 { 49 or 7 × 7 to the Pentecost.

7 to Whitsun-week, and the Pentecostal Dove.

The old Chaldean solar year of —— 360 days.

The Typical Structure of the Greek-Egyptian Dial with Steps, in Explanation of the Curves.

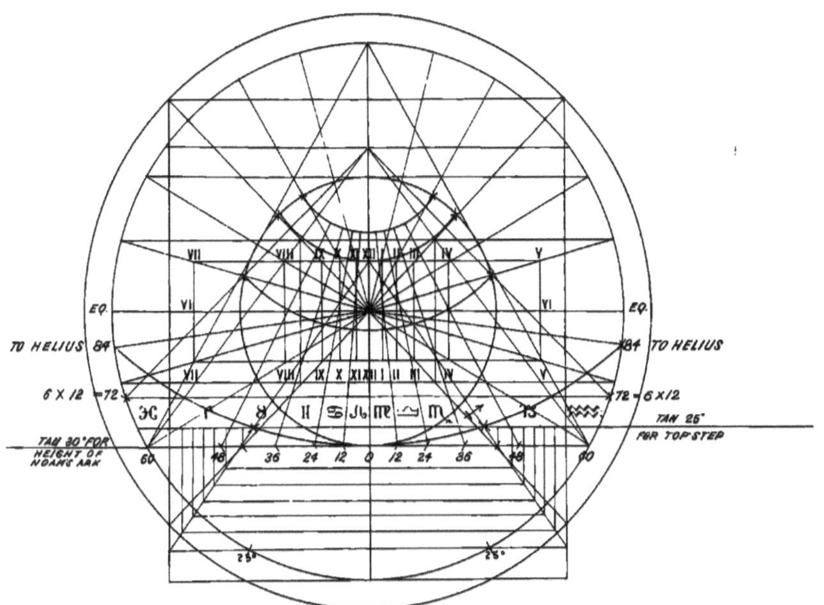

1st and Uppermost Curve cuts off from the Equinoctial 2 × 150 = 300 for 10 × 30 days.
or 2 × 135 = 270 for 10 × 27 days.

2d and Middle Curve cuts off " " 2 × 105 or 14 × 15° nearly as 12 × 18°.

3d and Lowest Curve cuts off 2 × 84 to Helius, reducible to, . . . } 10 × 14 = 140 for half of 280 or 10 × 28 days.
or 144 for 12 × 12 instead of 10 × 14.
or 120 as 12 × 10 = 8 × 15.

CORRECTED MODE OF COMPARING THE FRONT AND SIDE MEASUREMENTS OF A DIAL WITH STEPS,

For N. Lat. 54°, in Imitation of the Greek-Egyptian Dial with Steps, brought from Alexandria.

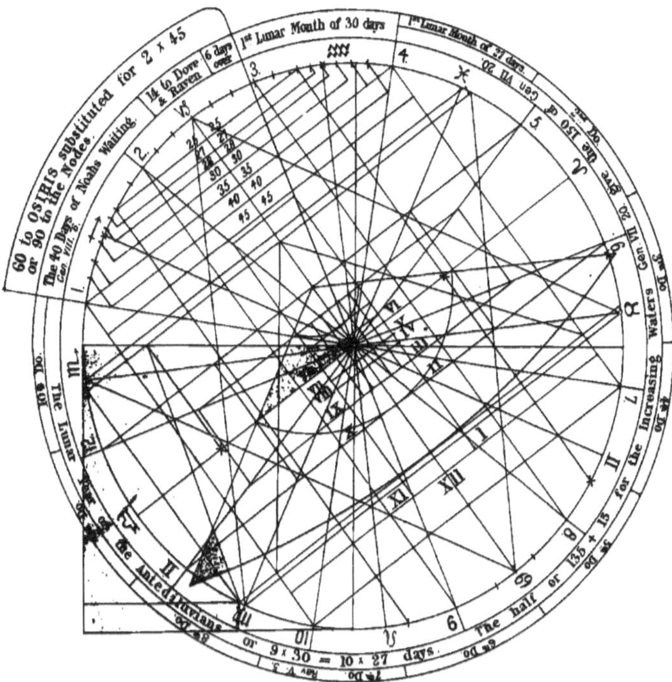

10 × 27 days, from the entrance of the Sun into Pisces to his exit from Scorpio, give nine old Chaldean months of thirty days to the first day of tenth month; whence we date the forty days of Noah's waiting, before he sent forth from his Ark the Raven and the Dove.

Thus that symbolism stands identified with the THOTH, or beginning of the old Egyptian year, from the full moon in Capricorn.

Note, also, that the lunar year of ten months, reckoned at twenty-seven days each, from 1° in ♓ to 30° in ♏ symbolised the beginning and end of typical and prophetic time to Vishnu's ten Avataras, as beginning from the Sun in Pisces, and ending with Scorpio; even as the death of Hercules (supposed to be the Bala-Rama of the Hindus) proceeded from the poisoned blood of Hydra.

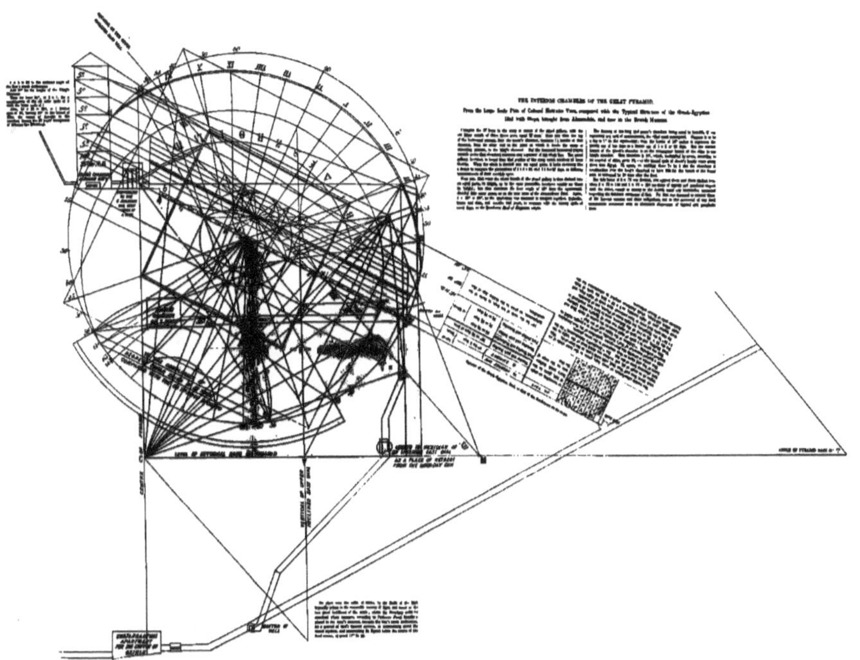
THE INTERIOR CHAMBERS OF THE GREAT PYRAMID.

LIST OF QUARTO ILLUSTRATIONS.

PART I.

A descriptive list of the first 38 will be found in the tract immediately following p. 62.

39. Stands as 1st of *three*, designed for friends at the British Museum. This is an explanation of the Greek-Egyptian Dial's structure, accompanied by a perspective representation of it as photographed in front, and on its west side, from the Model exhibited at Paris.

40. As 2d of the three for the British Museum. This illustrates the seven steps of the Greek-Egyptian Dial from the seven Dwipas of the ancient Hindu Philosophy.

41. As 3d and last of do. This divides the Equinoctial to a year of three seasons, represented by the three Avasthanas, *or great divisions*, numbering 27 asterisms in the philosophy of the ancient Hindus. By a metaphor from this, the most ancient division of their VEDA (or sacred book) numbered only *three* parts. Its division into four parts followed that of the Equinoctial to a year of 28 asterisms of 10° each, supplemented by 80 to Hydra, typically measuring the NODAL life of the Egyptian APHOPHIS, *by two days of* 40 *each.*

To the above the following *nine* were added for the binding in 1868; though not enumerated in the above mentioned list, which was printed long before the then binding of half-dozen copies, which stamped the state of progress at the Grosmont Confirmation in the April of 1868.

42-43. Differing Modifications of the East and West Quadrant Dial, in its typical relation to the Mythic History of Jason and Medea.

43. Ditto, compared with the Dragon symbolism of the Ancient Orientals, for the Moon's Nodes.

44. The Jambu Dwipa of the ancient Hindu Dialling Geography.

45. The Symbolic trees of Life and Knowledge.

46. Vishnu on his Porpoise, as Arion on his Dolphin.

47. Charon, in his Argonautic ferry boat; copied from a photograph of Spanish armoury, with allegorical designs of ancient history embossed thereon.

The collection in the British Museum amounts, I believe, to 92.

The above complete the illustrations of PART I. which terminates with page 104 of these Dialling tracts.

PART II.

1. The Hieroglyphic Frontispiece, with symbols of Assyrian and Egyptian origin.
2. The "Winged Disc," or Seraphic emblem of the ancient Egyptians, for the Meridian of their East and West typical Dialling. From Dr S. Birch's Egyptian Antiquities in the British Museum.
3. Egyptian Hieroglyphics, from a fragment of an Obelisk at Rome. From No. 3 to 5 (*b*) inclusive associates this stage of the thought with a visit to Cambridge in July 1868; whilst 5 (*b*) commemorates a visit to the Leed's Exhibition and Far-Headingly in the October following.

4. The Structure of the Greek-Egyptian Dial delineated as that of a direct South Dial by the late J. B. Smales, Esq., of St John's College, Cambridge.

5 (*a*) Ancient American Cross, from "Stephen's Central America," sketched by the late J. B. Smales, Esq.

5 (*b*) Christian and Phœnician symbols for the Cross with the mortuary emblems of heathen Rome, and a Mithraic emblem, from a MS., exhibited at Leeds, as belonging to the late Emperor Theodore of Abyssinia.

6. Heathen notions of the crucifixion, associated with the Christian doctrine of the resurrection, and the fruit of the tree of life restored to man in Christ. *See* Hepay's contributions from Rome to the "Art Journal."

7. The "eye of Providence," amongst the symbols on the Planisphere of Tentyra, given to that on the prow of a Chinese Junk. It is here grouped with the symbols of the old Egyptian Planisphere, as Noah's ark is with those on our own celestial globe; to mark the probable origin of the typical structure given to the ships of Tarshish, and to the sacred ships of the Egyptians, Greeks, and other Orientals, as derived from their traditions respecting Noah's ark. *See* also Plate XVI.

8. Diagram to illustrate the relation of Israel's midnight darkness in Egypt, to the 40 years of wandering in the wilderness by which it was followed, before being led northward by Joshua, *into the land of Israel's promised rest.* This was thus symbolised *as the rest of a people called children of light and of the day*, in contrast to the people of an outer world, symbolised as remaining in darkness and the shadow of death, after the Exodus of Israel out of Egypt. *The consummation of that Exodus being reserved for Joshua, the type of Christ, man's* SUN OF RIGHTEOUSNESS (after a wandering in the wilderness *southward* for 40 years under the guidance of Moses and Aaron), was thus symbolised to the Sun's North Declination; *as to ascending light eastward going north* from the Vernal Equinox, for the summer season.

9. Professor Smyth's vertical section of the great Pyramid, etc.

10. The Varshas and Mountains of the earth, spanned by the Lotus symbolism for the earth, on a Quadrant of the Equinoctial, for a measure of the week of 9 days, to the diurnal arc of their east and west typical dialling, in the philosophy of the ancient Hindus.

11 (*a*.) Manetho's XXX Dynasties.

11 (*b*.) The 50 Sons of Egyptus and 50 daughters of Danaus numbered eastward and westward to the north and south—like the Dove and Raven of the Jews—compared with the Lion and Unicorn of our national arms, for symbolisms of ascending and descending light, on the east and west quadrant dialling of the ancient Orientals.

Note also the reference of the same symbolism to the difference of form in which Joseph sought the blessing of Jacob on Ephraim and Manasseh, in contrast to that of the typical form chosen by Jacob, and compare Psalm lxxxi. 3, 4.

12. Another form of adapting our national emblem of the Lion and Unicorn to the Dove and Raven of the Jews, on an east and west Quadrant Dial.

13. The typical structure of a Chinese junk with the "eye of Providence" on its prow, compared with the east and west quadrant dialling arc of typical account, amongst the ancient Orientals.

14 (*a*). The old Saxon Dials at Kirkdale and Edstone, Yorkshire.

14 (*b*). An East and West Dial for 12 hours of Enoch, as hours of 80 minutes to 20 degrees of the Equinoctial, in explanation of the lines on the Saxon Dials.

15. The hour-lines of a Babylonian Dial, as constructed by Ferguson for London.

16. Gnomons for Dialling by a point of light, and point of shadow.

17. Inclined Dial Planes from Bedos de Cellos.

18. Meridians from Bedos de Cellos for Horizontal, South Vertical, and Declining Dial Planes.

19. The Geometric Structure of the Greek Egyptian Dial compared with the fundamental Diagram in the Dialling of Sylvanus Morgan.

20. To keep the hour-lines of a Declining Dial within a right-angled parallelogram, by Sylvanus Morgan.

21-24. The relation of the steps to the curves of the Greek-Egyptian Dial, illustrated from the Dialling of Sylvanus Morgan.

25. The astronomical pillar in the Court of Art, by Sylvanus Morgan.

26. Female Symbol for our earthly Sphere, from Sylvanus Morgan.

27-34. Various attempts to illustrate the structure of the Greek-Egyptian Dial with Steps, considered as the hollow semicircle of Babylonian origin, adapted to a Quadrant measure of Ascending and Descending Light by the ancient Egyptians.

35. The Hindu Zodiac for the week of 9 days (as $9 \times 40 = 360$), divided to the hour lines of an East and West Dial, for comparison with the East and West Dialling of Sylvanus Morgan, p. 55.

36. The two Dials at Sleights' Church, near Whitby.

37. The Vertical Declining Dial, by the Bridge, on entering Lofthouse from Whitby.

38. The Theatre of MACAO from a *small* photograph purchased at an Exhibition in Pall Mall, London, of Chinese scenery in a Gallery of water-coloured paintings by Hildebrandt, 1865. My reason for allowing this to be grouped amongst the other Illustrations of Oriental Dialling account, is a conviction that all ancient theatricals were more or less associated with their early traditions of religion, even as the theatres of the Greeks and Romans were identified with the worship of Bacchus, their Sun-God.

39 *and* 40. New designs for the outside Wrappers, No. 39, for the Octavo volume, compares the symbolic Tree of Life (found amongst the old Assyrian Sculptures at Khorsabad), with the decorated Cross of the mediæval Christian Church, as symbols of a common typical origin astronomically.

40. For the Quarto volume may be explained as below, in its relation to the flaming sword of Gen. iii. 24:

The horizon in this case is a parallel to the water-level of the Nile in Piazzi Smyth's Meridian section of the great Pyramids.

The intersection of the Meridian by the Equator and Earth's Axis on the Horizon explains the source of the metaphor used in the "*flaming sword*," which turns every way to guard the way of the Tree of Life—as to God's keeping—as the light of life to man: Gen. iii. 24.

Thus the ancient Hindus accounted for the contrast of Waters looking dark by day and light by night, because the waters covered the sun by night which returned to Earth by day.

See the Vishnu Purana, p. 220.

South Declination to the Moon's Descending Node, eastward and westward for the hours of a Horizontal Dial, giving the hour of XII., Northward on the Horizon to Midday—though that of Midnight on an East and West Dial.

The *Evening* of the primeval day, typically gave the Moon's entrance into her Descending Node, westward in VIRGO, to the beginning of the Sun's South Declination from the Equator.	The *Morning* of the primeval day typically gave the Moon's entrance into her Ascending Node westward in LEO, to the Sun's entrance into his North Declination eastward in Pisces, *for the old year of three seasons*, numbering (in lunar form) 27 asterisms of 10° each from VIRGO.

Full Moon to Midnight.

6th Day.	7th Day.	2d Day.	3d Day.
9. Friday. ♀ Venus.	8. Saturday. ♄ Saturn.	7. Monday. ☽ Moon.	6. Tuesday. ♂ Mars.

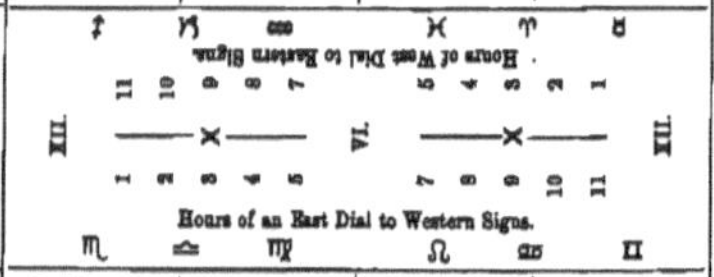

♐ ♑ ♒ ♓ ♈ ♉

Hours of West Dial to Eastern Signs.

11 10 9 8 7 5 4 3 2 1

XII. ——×—— VI. ——×—— XII.

1 2 3 4 5 7 8 9 10 11

Hours of an East Dial to Western Signs.

♏ ♎ ♍ ♌ ♋ ♊

2. Thursday. ♃ Jupiter.	3. Descending ☋ Node.	4. Ascending ☊ Node.	5. Wednesday. ☿ Mercury.
5th Day.	Nodes Going out.		4th Day.

New Moon to Midday.

North Declination to Moon's ascending Node, eastward and westward; for the hours of a South Vertical Dial, giving the Noonday hour of XII. southward to the Horizon.

Hence the meaning of the Mount of Olives, being typically divided towards the four winds of heaven, is that the influences of Christ's "*everlasting Gospel*" should thus pervade the earth therefrom.

The 6 months of the sun's south declination, given typically to our Lord's descent into Hell (as the Hades of the Greeks) as a symbolism for the grave under a two-fold reference: 1st, As an Elysium to the spirits of the blessed; 2d, As a place of never-ending torment to the condemned of man's judgment, which was the case of Christ's death, until reversed of God with eternal glory in the power of His resurrection.

But that was RESERVED for a typical teaching from the Sun's North Declination given to commemorate God's harvest mercies to man.

The reason was because the generation to whom the Gospel was first preached (at the sound of the *seventh trumpet, or that of the harvest month*), knew not how God's harvest-symbols of bread and wine were ordained to be an annually-renewable memorial in Christ (John vi. 48) that God willed mercy rather than sacrifice.

For the law of ceremonial sacrifices was one of *restricted application to the typical kingdom of Jewish nationality in the land of the Canaanite. See* Daniel xii.

The only sacrifice under God's new covenant of mercy, to both the houses of Israel, throughout their dispersions amongst the Gentiles, is that of self-humiliation for sin, *looking to God for grace unto redemption from its bondage in righteousness*: as God's appointed law of life, common both to Jew and Gentile in Christ.

The 6 months of the sun's north declination to the "6 water pots of of stone, containing 2 or 3 firkins a-piece (John ii. 6), after the manner of the purifying of the Jews."

These symbolise the effects of dew and rain, in their fertilising influences on earth, for the interval between spring-time and harvest, *to the use of water as a symbol of* Regeneration in Baptism.

Their conversion into wine, *at the marriage-feast of Cana in Galilee* (when the *seventh new moon*, as that of the autumnal equinox, *typically* numbered 3 days to 6 months, from the full moon of the vernal equinox), brings us to our harvest commemoration of God in the Lord's supper, as an indication that He willed mercy rather than sacrifice (Matt. xii. 7; Psalm lxxxi. 3, 4; Matt. xiii. 39). The atonement *of seven days* (Exod. xxix. 37) made that of *a seven years' cycle in the week of 7 years*, for confirming God's covenant with many (Dan. ix. 27).

We must here remark that the *seventh Jewish month of 28 days began in the sixth zodiacal sign*, which measured the distance from the new to the full moon, and inversely.

This illustrates the seven stars in the angel's *righthand*. When reckoning from the Winter Tropic Eastward to the vernal Equinox for the *Messianic beginning* of typical and prophetic time (Rev. i. 16).

With the above compare the miracles of the loaves and fishes:

John vi. 9, 13. The *five* loaves of the *five thousand* leaving *twelve* baskets of fragments.	Matthew xv. 34-38. The *seven* loaves of the *four thousand*, leaving *seven* baskets of fragments.

The above reference to the changing of water into wine at the marriage-feast in Cana of Galilee, reminds me of an epigram I remember having seen in my schoolboy-days, at St Paul's, London; but whether as an old tradition, or as the translation of a senior schoolboy from the words, "The modest water saw the Lord and blushed," in a then well-known child's book, called "Edward Manderville," I cannot say. The last line is all that I can remember of the Latin epigram, whilst convinced that there was at least one other. I have therefore roughly completed the distich to connect the beautifully-expressed latter line, which I distinctly remember, with its subject:

Nuptis numen adest; lympharum vasa* parantur;
"Conscia lympha Deum vidit et † erubuit."

* The six water pots, after the manner of the purification of the Jews, holding *two* or *three* firkins a-piece, symbolise the 6 months of the sun's north declination divided to 12 half-months, compared with 12 equinoctial hours, or divided to months of 8 weeks each, for the semi-equinoctial of 180, measured by the 18 Ethiopians of Herodotus.

† As an allegory or parable of similarly moral significance, *see* Proverbs xv. 16, 17.

The East and West *typical* dialling of the ancient orientals, thus considered, unfolds to us the origin of the metaphor used in Zechariah's typical prophecy, respecting a day *then known only to the Lord*, viz., that of Messiah's advent, in a cloudy and dark day—the day of the heathen;—as a day in which it should not be clear or dark until *the evening, which dated the beginning of Lunar typical time from the Sun's South Declination.*

Thus God's two witnesses (His Word, and His Works personified in Christ) prophesied in sackcloth for 1260 days preceding the Crucifixion of Christ as Messiah. That was at the Passover in the midst of a week of seven years, reckoned from 7th month to 7th month, as from harvest to harvest; from atonement to atonement; or from *New* Moon to *New* Moon; divided in the half by the Paschal *full* moon. Compare Eph. iv. 9, 10, with Rev. xi. 3 : xii. 14.

But the Sun's South Declination for the old year of three seasons was then given to the Moon's descending node in VIRGO. His North Declination (made to symbolise Messiah's resurrection glory) was, on the other hand, given to the Moon's ascending node in LEO; whilst the Sun's North Declination would be reckoned *Eastward to the rising sun*, as the position assigned for the encampment of JUDAH, before their typical tabernacle.

Thus we trace the source of the metaphor used in the typical prophecy relating to Messiah's birth of a pure *Virgin*, to identify his Advent with the pure Gospel teaching of a Reformed Jewish Church, in contrast to that which had been previously teaching the fear of God only by the precept of man. Hence the phraseology of Jewish typical prophecy, discriminating between the idolatrous tendencies of both the houses of Israel, under the personifications of AHOLAH and AHOLIBAH (Ezek. xxiii.); and the life-preserving energy of a purer faith, as the strength of Judah against Sennacherib in Hezekiah's day, saying of the Assyrian, "The VIRGIN, the *daughter of Zion*, hath laughed thee to scorn."

We must here, also, remember that the position assigned to the encampment of EPHRAIM with BENJAMIN before their typical tabernacle, was Westward to the setting Sun; in contrast to that of JUDAH Eastward to the rising Sun: whilst Messiah's Advent was predicted *as the rising of the SUN of RIGHTEOUSNESS with healing on his wings.*

This, moreover, serves to illustrate the typical ordinance for the division of the land to the 12 tribes in the day of their return from Babylon, viz., *seven* to Judah, Eastward and Westward to the North; and five to Benjamin, Eastward and Westward to the South of the Holy Oblation in Ezekiel's vision of typical prophecy.

The old week of 8 days, as 8 × 45° = 360, was reduced to one of 8 = 40 = 320; as from that of 9 × 40 = 360 by omitting Sunday; because the Sun shines on all days. For it is clear that this was in fact the old week of 9 days, by Friday being numbered 9 thereon; but typically divided to their eight Regents of the sphere, *as to the Cycle of their new moons. See* the observation of Mr E. Sang, Edinburgh, on the 11,341 years of Herod, considered as the days in 30 solar years, or 31 Lunar years in 32 years, each numbering 12 lunations of 29d. 12h. 42m. mean time, or 354d. 8h. 48m. yearly.

This also explains how Thursday was the *second* day of the week when beginning from *Jupiter to the Conjunction of the Sun* and Moon Westward in VIRGO, as from the beginning of the Sun's South Declination to the Moon's descending Node (Ketu) on that Zodiac. When Thursday to Jupiter was numbered 5th day in a week of 7 or 9 days beginning from Sunday, the beginning of that week was given Eastward to the Sun's North Declination, and the Moon's ascending node (RAHU) *beginning his quadrant circuit from the Sun to the Moon and back again in LEO on that Zodiac.* Hence the celebrated Lion *Jos* of the Chinese and other orientals divided into pairs for Ascending and Descending light. Captain W. H. Marwood, of the Artillery Volunteer Corps, Whitby, brought with him from China *two* of these *Joses*, or Nodal symbols, for their DIESPATER or daily providence. On one of these the Lion has his paw upon a dog, as if subdued; but on the other the dog seems to be baiting the Lion. The Dog I take to be a symbol for *the Dog star in Cancer, the Zodiacal sign next before Leo.*

He brought also with him, from China, another symbolic group of figures, one of which got broken on the road, and its place is supplied by a *Budha* or *Ganesha*, or the Hindu Janus, from the Elephant's proboscis thereon. From this, therefore, no opinion can be formed as to the meaning of the group; all of which, with one exception, are carved in soap stone. The one exception is a *black* figure, forming one in a group of *seven*; with a group of *three* below. The centre of these three is as a Child on or seated by a Dragon. He tells me that is a symbol of very great esteem amongst them; and I think it probably of the same significance as the HORUS of the Ancient Egyptians, between ISIS and OSIRIS; viz., as the Man in the Moon, when first appearing in infant form, near the place of the new Moon; before beginning his reign of 20 days in the first lunation of the year, as in all the rest, making 12 × 20 or 240* for his reign of Lunar light yearly, when the

* 240 + 60 made up their Noah's ark Lunar year of 300 days, as 300 + 60 made up their typical and prophetic Solar year of 360 days.

supplement of 240 to 360, or 120, was limited over the diurnal arc for man's day on their East and West typical Dialling, as in Gen. vi. 3, for 120 lunar years of 300 days to 100 old Chaldean solar years of 360 days.

The one *Black symbol* was probably the NITOCRIS of Herodotus, or the Queen of the 18 Ethiopians, numbered to the celebrated oriental cycle of the 330 kings.

For this Cycle numbered a year of *eleven* months to a day of *eleven* hours. Hence, on the hollow semicircle of the ancient Babylonians, reckoning 12 hours from sunrise to sunset, with the XII. o'clock hour of a polar dial reckoned as their *sixth*; it was typically numbered to the hour going out at XII. on an East and West Dial, but at VI. on a polar dial. Hence the sixth hour, as that of the Crucifixion, is called in Luke the hour of the Jewish Church, and the power of darkness.

For the 18 Ethiopians were 18 planetary cycles of 5 to the Quadrant of 90; or 18 Lunar Asterisms of 10°, each for 18 weeks of 10 days measured over the semicircle of 180; as given to the Sun's North Declination for six zodiacal signs, from the Vernal to the Autumnal Equinox, *extended by one from the Sun's South Declination to complete a summer season of seven months*, numbered on the centre of their typical dialling, (as in Isa. xxx. 26), to the Jewish Pentecostal Cycle of 7 × 7 for the Divine age of 5 × 10.

The Planetary Calendarium for the week of 8 days, by which the ancient Orientals divided the Equinoctial to their 8 regents of sphere, for 8 × 45 = 360, compared with a week of 9 days numbering 9 × 40; and subsequently reduced to one of 8 × 40, numbered 8 times for the 2 months extending over 64 days, during which Krishna and Bala Ramar (as the Sun and Moon, for the sun between his tropics to the Moon between her nodes) practised their military exercises in the Gymnasium of SANDIPANI (*See* Vishnu Purana, p. 561). The two months in this case supplemented the old Lunar year of 300 days to Enoch's solar year of 364 days, numbering 13 lunations of 28 days.

Similarly their celebrated cycle of 330 kings seems to commemorate the time when the zodiacal angles began to be reckoned at 24 (for $23\frac{1}{2}$ omitting the fraction) instead of at 25°, as supplemented by the 65 of Isaiah vii. 8. For 66, the complement of 24, multiplied by their planetary cycle of 5, give the 330 exactly.

We see thus also how their month of 32 days, formed from the old Egyptian week of 8 days, gave rise to a Lunar year of 10 months numbering 320 days. Hence the solar season of *two such months together, numbering 64 days*, which the Hindus dedicated to Krishna and Bala Rama.

The hour and day and month and year of Rev. ix. 15, associates the hour of darkness, *as the sixth of their typical time*, with the Nodal idolatry of the old Baalists, which was based on the old Chaldean solar year of 360 days. This they divided between a Lunar year of ten months and a *solar season of two months, typically divided between ascending and descending light, as between the moon's two nodal days; one of which, the first born to descending light, was fated to go out before the rising power of ascending light.* Thus "the hour of the Jewish Church and power of darkness" (Luke xxii. 53) refers to the Crucifixion of Christ *as a consequence of those idolatrous superstitions to which importance was attached* by the Rulers of the Jewish people, when Caiaphas said to his opponents, "Ye know nothing at all, nor consider that *it is expedient for us that one man should die for the people, and that the whole nation perish not.*" The explanation of the text is,—"And this spake he not of himself: *but being high priest* that year, *he prophesied that Jesus should die for that nation.*" This requires careful consideration. For it means not that he prophesied truly and in fulfilment of a righteous inspiration; *but that he, as high priest, having reputation amongst the people as a prophet commissioned of God by Moses, made a wrong and superstitious use of the reasoning faculties given him by God, when he confounded their typical law relating to the Scape goat, with the Gladiatorial decision between right and wrong, morally, in obedience to which it was necessary that one of the parties must die, except by some almost miraculous interposition in favour of the vanquished one. The idea was borrowed from the sixth hour of a Polar dial, or the twelfth of an East or West Dial, going out in the division of typical time, between Ascending and Descending light thereon.* For the 12 hours of their typical day were thus reduced to a Cycle of eleven, dedicated to the 330 Kings of the ancient Orientals, as impersonations of the nation's *Diespater*, daily for the old Chaldean year of 360 days less one month. Enoch's solar year numbered 365, according to (Gen. v. 23), though reckoned as 364 in the Ethiopian astronomy of Enoch, translated by Richard Laurence, LL.D., Archbishop of Cashel, and late Professor of Hebrew in the University of Oxford. Published by J. W. Parker, Oxford, MDCCCXXXVII.

The typical structure of the Greek Egyptian Dial with Steps was certainly framed to combine *a Lunar Calendarium for devotional purposes*, with their dialling Chronicle of passing solar time.

Howsoever they might vary the planetary dedication for the *first hour and day, etc., of this typical Dialling, it always* compared a day of 30 Muhurttas with a month of 30 days, dividing their *Muhurttas* and *days* into six planetary Cycles of *five*, for five, six, and seven months, etc., etc.

Their Dial with Steps was a *Quadrant Universal Dial for* 45°, inclined Eastward at an angle of 28° for Horeb; when substituting Jewish months of 28 days, or 4 × 7, for the old Chaldean months of 30 days, divided into three weeks of 10 days monthly; for 9 weeks of 10 days to 10 weeks of 9 days to the Quadrant of 90. Thus they measured also 9 months of 30 days to 10 of 27 days; for the Cycle of their Lunar year, as ending in Haggai II., with the *ninth* month; but at other times with the *tenth month as commemorated by the ancient Romans in the word December*.

It appears also that the typical structure of the Greek-Egyptian Dial will explain the perplexed passage already quoted from page 484 of the Vishnu Purana in Tract, p. 89 of this volume.

My friend Mr James Wood agrees with me in thinking that the only intelligible meaning for the words, "When the two first stars of the great bear (viz., the two pointers *Dubhe* and *Merak*) *rise in the heavens, and some Lunar asterism is seen at night at an equal distance between them, is to conceive that they speak the language of an astronomical observation originally made for the Latitude of Tentyra* 26°, or of the Pyramid plain 30°, or by Moses for the Jews before Horeb in N. Lat. 28°. For the Horizon could not be *cut by a line passing midway between them, unless it represented the circle of perpetual light, for a latitude near 26° or 28°*

Thus for lat. 28° Mr Wood estimates that the angle between the meridian, or the hour circle, cutting the Horizon near the *Circle* passing midway between the pointers would be 18° or 20°. Either angle has much typical significance, that of 18° (or Pheron's hour) being the measure of twilight. That of 20 for the beginning of the Sun's right ascension from Aries, made the angle beyond which Eclipses could not occur, a measure of 10 for Sunday to the Sun on the Equator, divided equally between ascending light to the Sun's North Declination, and Descending light to the Sun's South Declination.

By Lunar Asterisms we learn, from the Vishnu Purana, p. 226, that they meant weekly lunar circuits of 9 days in months of 27 days for a lunar year of 270 days supplemented by 90 to the Nodes. This form of the lunar year, they began from the *Lunar asterism called the Aswins, in the Zodiacal sign Libra.* Their Lunar year of 280 days had for its *first Lunar Asterism Crittica in Virgo.* This form of the Lunar year was supplemented to 360 by 80 to APHOPHIS (a Sun Pharaoh) for two Nodal days of 40.* If therefore the Equinoctial was divided to the lunation of 30 days, and also to the Sun's right ascension beginning from Aries, *for the first New Moon of the Year, the point in which a circle passing mid way between the pointers at rising would cut* the horizon in an angle of 18° or 20° would be in Crittica the *third Lunar asterism of 9° from the Aswins.* The remaining in that conjunction for 100 years of men, would be for 10 days in the month of 30 days. This week of 10 days they measured by a chord of 120 to ⅓ of 360 yearly. This darkening of the heavens for *ten* days (as *then* limited over the monthly approach of the Moon to the Sun) gives the source of the Metaphor used in the going down and return of the Shadow by 10 degrees on the steps of AHAZ.

THE *THREEFOLD* LUNAR CALENDARIUM OF THE ANCIENT ORIENTALS, WITH ITS PLANETARY *DEDICATIONS* FOR THE DAYS OF THE WEEK.

These dedications for the days of the week originally followed the numbering of the planets in the order of their orbits (See Cicero's Som. Scip., cap. iv.), *beginning from Saturn the outermost*, and taking its cycle of 30 years for the basis of a typical comparison between the old Chaldean Solar year of 360 days, and their monthly Lunar year of 30 *days*, numbered to the cycle of their *new* moons as days of years. This may throw a light upon *the circular shrine provided by Manetho for deifying the ancient kings of Egypt to the extent of 30 dynasties.*

The *second* to Jupiter, shows why Jupiter was numbered as second day in a week, which numbered *all its days as beginning in the moon's descending node, for the evening before the morning of their primeval day.* For when *Sunday* to the sun beginning his north declination from the Vernal Equinox was made the *first* day of the week, Thursday to Ascension Day became the *fifth*, which was the place of *Wednesday* on the old Hindu Zodiac, which numbered Thursday to Jupiter for descending light to the *second* day of the week. Hence on their typical Quadrant Dialling for the Cycle of 5 beginning from Jupiter. Wednesday (dedicated to Mercury as the Caduceus bearer of Jupiter) *notified the turning point between ascending and descending weekly Lunar light.* This explains how *the Ember Days*, Wednesday, Friday, Saturday, *where made to notify the beginning of the four seasons, equally from descending lunar light, for all seasons of the year.* See the

* Hence the division for the steps, which explains *the going down and return of the shadow on the steps of Ahaz by 10 degrees*, sets off these 10 on the quadrant of 90 to the top step, for the Sunday to the Sun on the Equator, *ruling over the other six planetary days of the week*, divided equally between ascending and descending light (like the six days of creation, Gen. i.), as between two nodal days of 40 each, 6 lunar asterisms of 13 and *one third each*; for Enoch's 7 × 13 = 91 for 90. This fact I have proved to my own satisfaction this morning, 27th February 1870.

Calendarium of the Ancient Christian Church in the Preface to our Book of Common Prayer. Thus *also* they typified Monday, Tuesday, and Wednesday to ascending lunar light, *over their dialling are for Man's day* (measured by the 120 of Jonah's journey of 3 days across the great city NINEVEH) *whilst typifying its culminating glory to Holy Thursday, or ascension day, as to the beatified spirits of their dead.* Thus as the Orbit of Saturn was made a basis for comparing their monthly lunar year of 30 days, with their solar year of 360 days; so was the twelve years' Cycle of Jupiter taken for a basis when dividing *their planetary day to 30 Muhurttas of 12° each, or 48 minutes to a planetary hour when comparing their day of 30 Muhurttas with their month of 30 days.*

Thus we arrive at the first two stages in the construction of their "*Magnus Annus,*" by multiplying the orbits of the planets into one another. For the next was Mars, whose Cycle of nearly two years increased by TWO for the orbits of Venus and Mercury shows how the ancient Egyptians framed their great Sothiac period of 4 × 360=1440 days of years. This they also called their *lustrum* or 5 years' Cycle for 5 Lunar years of 280 days in 1400 days.

Next in order came the Sun (viz., as next to Mars, but with varied relation to Venus and Mercury), to whom we find they thus dedicated their great Sothiac Cycle of 1440 typical years. These multiplied by their Lunar year of 300 days produced their "great year" or Cycle of 432,000 mythic years, symbolised as years equally over the seconds of time in 5 days of 24 hours as over 1200 Solar years of 360 days, estimated also as 1200 monthly Lunar years to their historic sæculum of 100 years.

To the Sun in the Moon's Descending Node, as in South Declination from Thursday to Monday. — To the Sun in the Moon's Ascending Node, as in North Declination from Sunday to Thursday.

Their fixed Cœlum, or Heaven, the primum mobile of the 9 planetary orbs. Som. Scip. cap. iv.	Cœlum.	Saturn.	Jupiter.	Mars.	Central Sun to Mars & Venus between the Moon's Nodes.	Venus to	Mars.	Mercury to the Sun.	Moon.	
	1	2	3	4		5	6	7	8	9
Or thus numbered to their Calendarium.		1	2	3		4	5	6	7	—

Earth the ninth and lowest of their planetary orbits, but of no account to their Lunar Calendarium. This therefore answers to the JAMBU DWIPA of the ancient Hindus.

	♄	♃	☋	☉	☊	♂	☉	♀	☿	☽	
Saturday	7	5	3	1	6	3	1	6	4	2	Monday.
Sunday	1	6	4	2	7	4	2	7	5	3	Tuesday.
Monday	2	7	5	3	1	5	3	1	6	4	Wednesday.
Tuesday	3	1	6	4	2	6	4	2	7	5	Thursday.
Wednesday	4	2	7	5	3	7	5	3	1	6	Friday.
Thursday	5	3	1	6	4	1	6	4	2	7	Saturday.
Friday	6	4	2	7	5	2	7	5	3	1	Sunday.
Saturday	7	5	3	1	6	3	1	6	4	2	Monday.
Sunday	1	6	4	2	7	4	2	7	5	3	Tuesday.
Monday	2	7	5	3	1	5	3	1	6	4	Wednesday.
Tuesday	3	1	6	4	2	6	4	2	7	5	Thursday.
Wednesday	4	2	7	5	3	7	5	3	1	6	Friday.

Here we have 12 Cycles of 5 × 10=50; as the 7 × 7=49 of Jewish Pentecostal reckoning, for a Lunar Calendarium dividing 600 days of years typically between day and night, measured to ascending and descending light on the centre of their East and West Quadrant Dialling by the two Zodical angles, estimated at 25° each.

This will illustrate the 600 years of Noah's life preceding the flood, as typically numbered to the days and nights in their *then Lunar year of* 300 NYCHTHEMERA.

But they seem also to have divided this Calendarium unequally; viz., as 6 Cycles of 5 taken 12 times to make up their Solar year of 360 days. The remaining 4 Cycles of 5 they also numbered 12 times to the longest day of 240 in the astronomy of the ancient Enoch.

If, however, we divide the 12 days of this Calendarium into seven days on the one hand, as $7 \times 50 = 350$ to the Post diluvian age of Noah's life, we obtain for the remainder of the Calendarium 5 days to be multiplied by 50, for a numbering of their Divine age over each day, made thus to represent a Cycle of 50 days, to the extent of 250° the number of the Censers which characterised the rebellion of Korah, Dathan, and Abiram, as of one which sought to make Israel apostatise to the renewed worship of the Nodes.

Now the typical year of the Jews was limited to a seed-time and harvest of *seven* months, in contradistinction to the old Baalistic division of the Solar year of 12 months, between a Lunar year of ten months and a Solar season of two months, thus numbering only six Planetary Cycles of five to each month of 30 days compared with a day of 30 Muhurttas, or planetary hours, we have $7 \times 30 = 210$ for the longest day in Palestine and the Pyramid plain, supplemented by $5 \cdot 30 = 150$, for the Winter season of their traditions relating to Noah and his Ark.

Thus omitting the Planetary symbol of ☉ on this Calendarium to identify the Solar glory with that of God's mercies daily renewed for all the days of the week, *as referred to in Isaiah* xxx. 26, we have seven days numbered conjointly to the sun and moon from two beginnings. The first was from Wednesday to Mercury, the second from Friday, dedicated to Venus, as the Great Diana of the Ephesians, whose image fell down from Jupiter, when the first *new moon* of the oldest Oriental year was numbered to the sun at the Winter Tropic, between ♏ and ♐. This form was followed in the Calendarium of the Mediaeval Christian Church, when numbering Wednesday, Friday, and Saturday as *ember* days to the beginning of each of the four seasons, as an ordinance framed for applying a lunar Calendarium to the quadrant measure of their East and West Dialling arc.

Compare Genesis xlvii. 2 on the five brethren of Joseph, with the South of the Holy Oblation, Ezek. xlviii. 22-28.

	☿	☽	♄	♃		☉	
Wednesday	4	2	7	5	3	1	Sunday
Thursday	5	3	1	6	4	2	Monday
Friday	6	4	2	7	5	3	Tuesday
Saturday	7	5	3	1	6	4	Wednesday
Sunday	1	6	4	2	7	5	Thursday

Mercury, the Caduceus bearer of Jupiter to the Sun in his south Declination for the half weekly Cycle of 5 days.

Compare Genesis xlvii. on the settlement of seven tribes northward in the land of Goshen with Ezek. xlviii. 1 9, and Isaiah xxx. 26.

Monday	2	7	5	3	1	6	Friday
Tuesday	3	1	6	4	2	7	Saturday
Wednesday	4	2	7	5	3	1	Sunday
Thursday	5	3	1	6	4	2	Monday
Friday	6	4	2	7	5	3	Tuesday
Saturday	7	5	3	1	6	4	Wednesday
Sunday	1	6	4	2	7	5	Thursday

Monday to the Moon going forth with the Sun in his North Declination: for the weekly lunar Cycle of seven days.

This Calendarium doubled, for 12 days of 12 hours, etc., substitutes the celebrated Jewish Cycle of $12 \times 12 = 144$ for the old Baalistic Cycle of $12 \times 10 = 120$, and as over Nineveh.

Sol ☉ Isaiah xxx. 26.

Genesis xlvii. 4 with Ezek. xlviii. 22-28.

	♀	☿	☽	♄	♃	♂	
Friday	6	4	2	7	5	3	Tuesday
Saturday	7	5	3	1	6	4	Wednesday
Sunday	1	6	4	2	7	5	Thursday
Monday	2	7	4	3	1	6	Friday
Tuesday	3	1	6	4	2	7	Saturday

Genesis xlvii. 4 with Ezek. xlviii. 1-9, and Isaiah xxx. 26.

Wednesday	4	2	7	5	3	1	Sunday
Thursday	5	3	1	6	1	2	Monday
Friday	6	1	3	7	5	3	Tuesday
Saturday	7	5	3	1	6	1	Wednesday
Sunday	1	6	4	2	7	5	Thursday
Monday	2	7	5	3	1	6	Friday
Tuesday	3	1	6	4	2	7	Saturday

Here we have Venus to Mars in the Sun's South Declination, when his North Declination dated its beginning typically from Wednesday to Mercury then in attendance on the Sun instead of Venus.

This may possibly refer to Venus being sometimes a morning, at others an evening star.

We must here remember that they who dedicated Thursday to Jupiter for the first day of the week to the *moons' descending node for Evening before morning began their reckoning for Thursday from Wednesday Evening.* Similarly, the Jews began their Saturday's *Sabbath* from the *Friday Evening;* and the Mediaeval Christian Church began the Lord's Day, which they dedicated to the Sun, as to Christ, man's SUN of Righteousness, from *Saturday* Evening. This may explain its selection of Wednesday, Friday, and Saturday, for its *Ember days to mark* the beginning of their typical and prophetic time from descending light to the moon's descending node *for the four seasons of the year.*

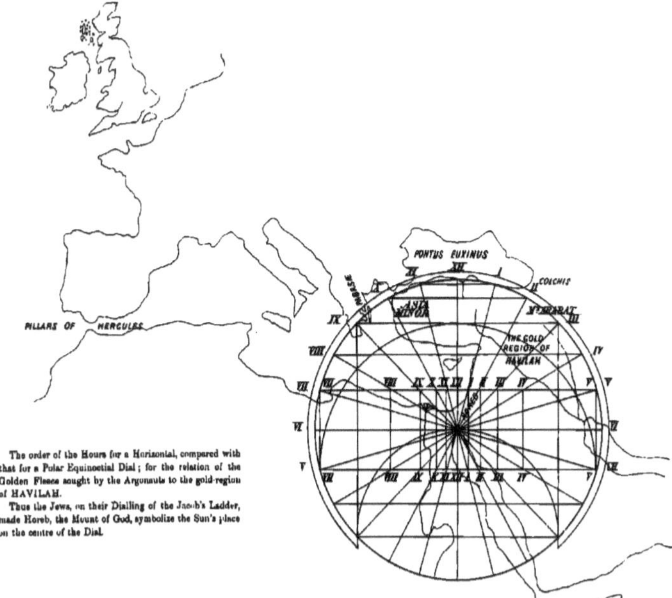

The order of the Hours for a Horizontal, compared with that for a Polar Equinoctial Dial; for the relation of the Golden Fleece sought by the Argonauts to the gold-region of HAVILAH.

Thus the Jews, on their Dialling of the Jacob's Ladder, made Horeb, the Mount of God, symbolize the Sun's place on the centre of the Dial.

The shaded part represents the base of the Dial when standing *vertically*, for a bird's eye form of the front view.

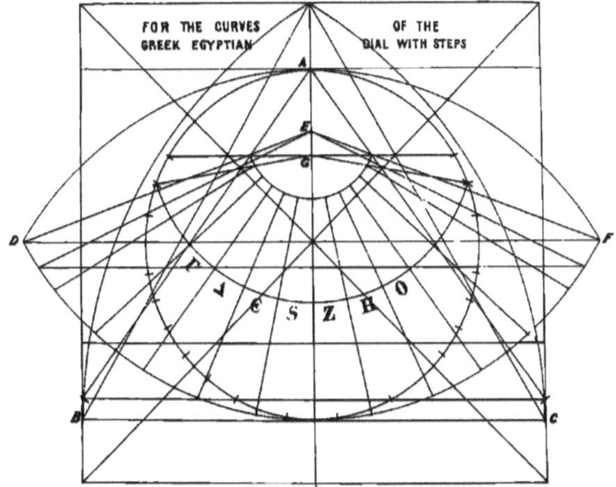

This front view was taken when the Dial was lying *horizontally* on its back.

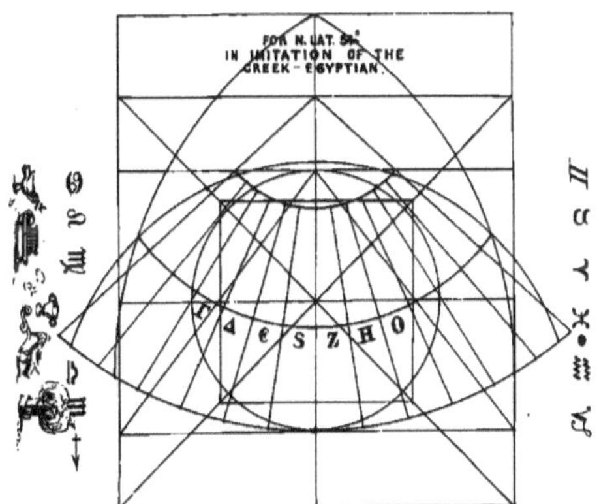

From the Model made for the Industrial Exhibition in 1866. The coloured square represents the relation of their four square City of Light to the equinoctial of an East and West or Polar Dial.

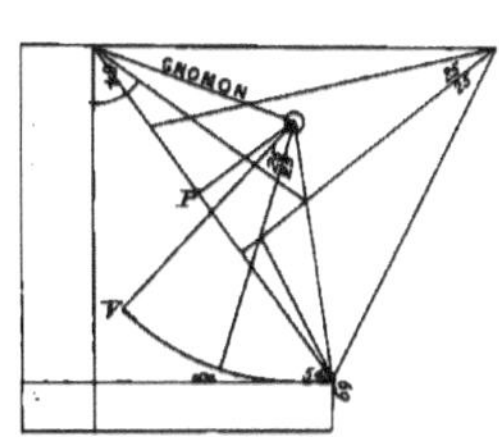

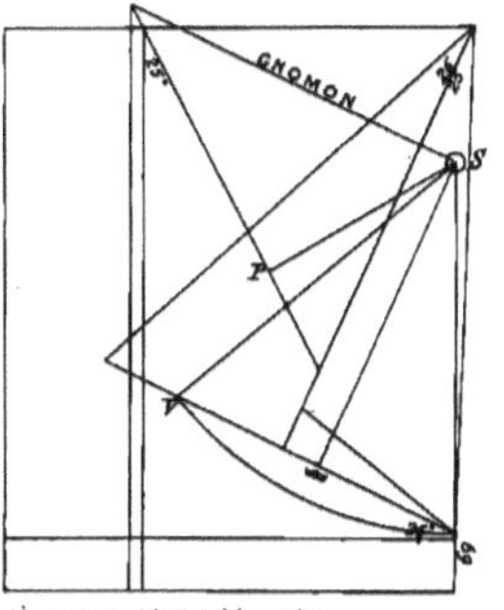

Direction & height of Gnomon given on a West side view.

THE CALENDARIUM ON THE GREEK-EGYPTIAN DIAL WITH STEPS, COMPARED WITH THAT OF THE CHRONOMÈTRE SOLAIRE, INVENTED AND PATENTED BY M. FLECHET, AT PARIS.

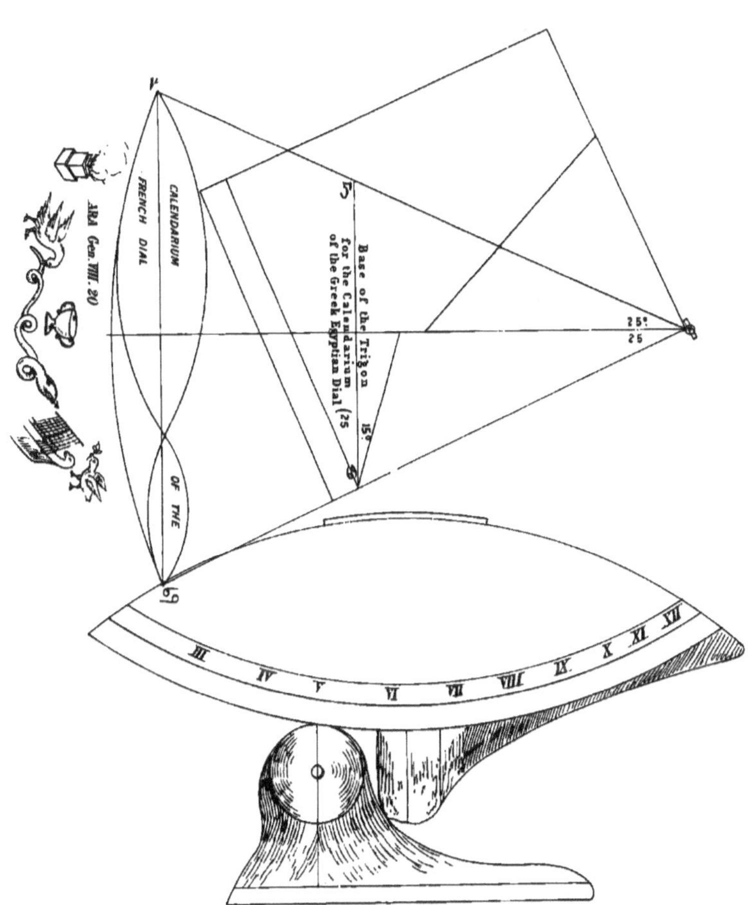

राशी:चक्र

Rāsi Chakra

The Hindu Zodiac, and Solar System

from Moor's Hindu Pantheon

TOMB 24 GHIZEH

SACRED BOAT OF PRINCE MOURHET

A CHINESE JUNK, WITH THE EYE OF PROVIDENCE THEREON.

THE BARIS, OR SACRED BOAT OF THE EGYPTIANS.

From the British Museum.

THE BARIS OR SACRED BOAT OF THE EGYPTIANS.

from the British Museum.

MITHRAIC GROUP.

From the British Museum

MITHRAIC GROUP WITH FIGURES REPRESENTING DAY & NIGHT.

From the British Museum.

THE ALEXANDRINE DIAL WITH STEPS, ON A FRONT VIEW,
Compared with a Hollow South Vertical for N. lat. 25°, constructed according to Fale's Rule.

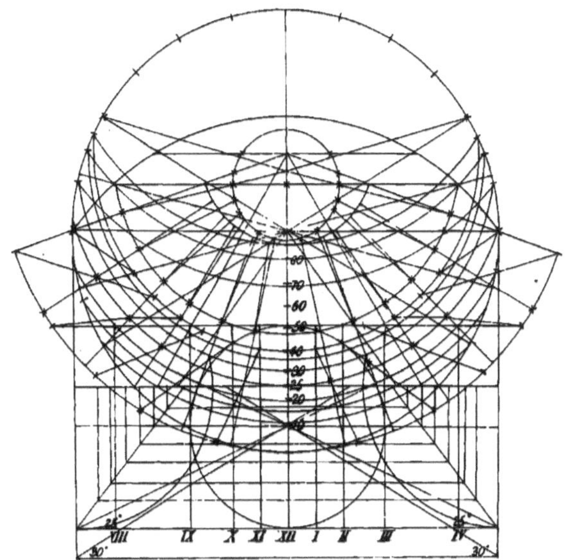

Though the typical features of these *three* Symbolisms will hold good, the division of the steps thereon to the Equinoctial is (I now think) faulty on all; as calculated for that radius of the Equinoctial by which I then determined *hypothetically* the direction and height of the Gnomon in each case. For this reason I have let them stand as illustrations, though not without this qualification,—that the radius for the small Equinoctial of the Polar Dial on the Front Steps must be the half of 83° or 84° to Helius—substituted for 45°, the half of 90°

THE STEPS OF THE GREEK-EGYPTIAN DIAL,

Numbered to *the different Oriental forms* of Calendaring the Days of the Week to the Hours of the Day.

1*st*, As beginning between Thursday and Friday, when reckoned Southward to the Descending Node, from the Sun's third gate, as by the Fakeers.

2*d*, As beginning from Sunday, when turning Northward from the Sun's *fourth* gate of Enoch's Astronomy, as made the beginning of typical time by the Sittaanders.

3*d*, Probably the Egyptian variation of No. 1, associating Wednesday as dedicated to Mercury (the Caduceus bearer of Jupiter), with the Lunar Calendarium of their Noah's Ark Symbolism, $4 \times 2 = 8$ hours to the centre of the Dial; for $\frac{120}{8}° = 15°$ to an hour of Equinoctial time.

$7 \times 6 = 42$, for 7 weeks of 6 days twice numbered, viz., Eastward and Westward on the side steps; by substituting the Egyptian Quadrant of 84° (as $2 \times 42 = 3 \times 48$ and 7×12), for the old Chaldean Quadrant of 90°.

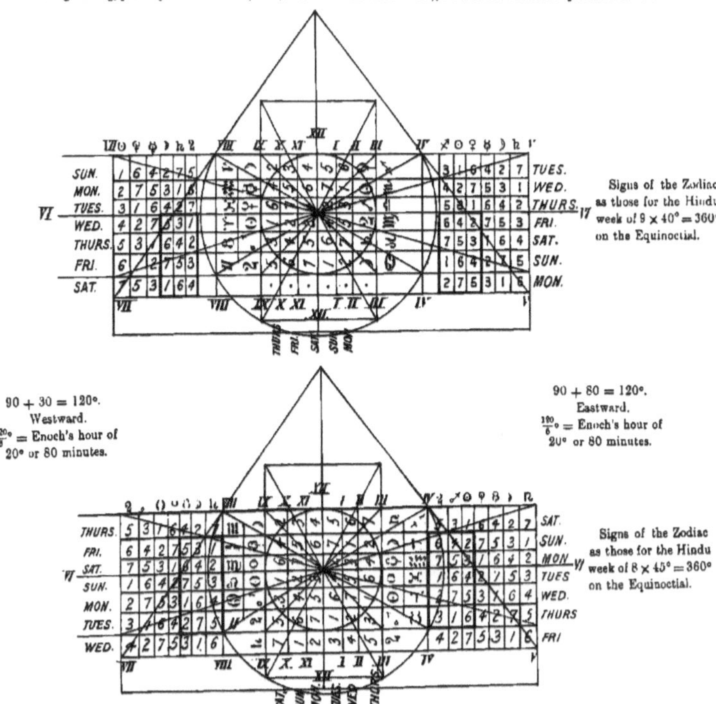

Thus the days of the week are numbered to the Planetary hours for morning and evening, as by Blundevil for the week of seven days, beginning from SUNDAY.

But they are numbered in cycles of 5, 6, or 7 to the Monthly Calendarium on the Centre, as to 6 cycles of 5, multiplied by 5 for 150, or half of 300 on the Calendarium of the Ham-shaped Dial.

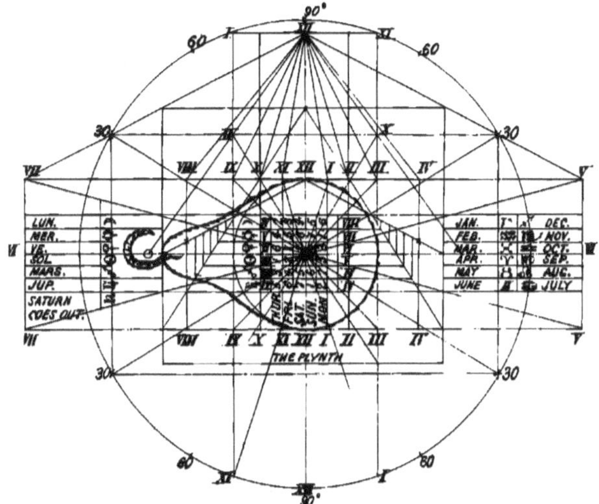

The 30 Cubits for the whole height of Noah's Ark, measured typically as Degrees of the Circle to the Boat Dialling of the Ancient Orientals.

Compare *this Dialling with Steps* for Whitby, N. lat. 54°, with the ancient Sun-Dial in the shape of a Ham, numbered 1568 in Knight's *Pictorial Gallery of Arts*, and the Sun-Dial with Portable Meridian in Blackie's *Popular Encyclopædia*, with *the Greek-Egyptian Dial with Steps* of the era of the Ptolemies, brought from the base of the Obelisk called Cleopatra's Needle, at Alexandria, and presented to the British Museum by John Scott Tucker, Esq.

N.B.—This Calendarium seems to prove what the Greeks meant by Jupiter dethroning Saturn, in their Cosmogony dating "a Jove principium."

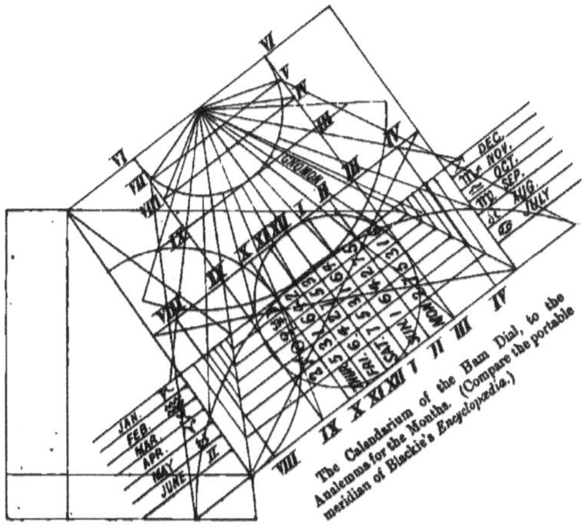

The Calendarium of the Bam Dial, to the Analemma for the Months. (Compare the portable meridian of Blackie's *Encyclopædia*.)

Relation of the West Side to the Front View of a Dial with Steps for Whitby (N. lat. 54°), in imitation of the Greek-Egyptian Dial with Steps, brought from Alexandria, and now in the British Museum. (Compare Herodotus, respecting the West End of the Temple of Vulcan, built by Rhampsinitus.)

Illustration for the Days of the Week, as differently numbered to the Equinoctial, on the two Zodiacs of the Hindus.

The numbering of the twelve tribes round the typical Sanctuary Psalm l. v. 1,—"The mighty God, even the Lord, hath spoken, and called the earth from the rising of the sun to the going down thereof." Compare Isaiah lix. 9, Matt. viii. 11, with Zech. xiv. 7, 8, in illustration of Gen. xxviii. 14, Psalm lxxv. 6.

	Simeon.	Reuben, 1st born near the THOTH of the Egyptians	Zebulun.	Issachar.	Judah to (Numbers ii. 3.) with Gen. 1·14 Sunrise	Benjamin.
Enoch's Eastern Gates of the Sun.	♐	♑	♒	♓	♈	♉
	1	2	3	4	5	6
The old Egyptian week of 8 days, from that of 9 days, as 8 × 45 = 360°.	9. FRI.	8. SAT.		7. MON.		6. TUES
	2. THURS.	3. N.D.		4. N.A.		5. WED
Enoch's Western Gates of the Sun.	1	2	3	4	5	6
	♏	♎	♍	♌	♋	♊
	Gad, a troop. Compare Rev. ii. 9, and ix. 10.	Naphtali to South-West. Deut. xxxiii. 23, Josh. xix. 34.	Asher.	DAN. The Judge. Gen. xlix. 16, Rev. v. 5.	Ephraim to West. Numbers ii. 18, and turning back in the day of battle. Psalm lxxviii. 9.	Manasseh.

Compare their order of march, Num. ii. 7, with that of ascending and descending light, as numbered to the *Central* SUN, on their East and West Dialling. This, moreover, illustrates Zech. xiv. 4, from Deut. xxvii. 12, 13; whence the imagery used in the Parable of Dives and Lazarus.

East to South for Descending Node.	Levites with Tabernacle.	West to North for Ascending Node.
Judah to East. Reuben to South.		Ephraim, West. DAN, North.

Enoch's Eastern Gates of the Sun.	♊	♉	♈	♓	♒	♑
	6	5	4	3	2	1
Our week of 7 days from that of 9 days, as 9 × 40 = 360°.	8. ASC. NODE	5. THURS.	1. SUNDAY	6. FRI.		3. TUES
	8	4. WED.	2. MONDAY.	7. SAT.	9 DESC. NODE	3
Enoch's Western Gates of the Sun.	6	5	4	3	2	1
	♋	♌	♍	♎	♏	♐

This second form of the week (by giving the North Ecliptic to the Western Horizon) *reverses the typical ordering of the tribes, as numbered to the 4 Cardinal points of the horizon by Moses.*

May not this have something to do with *the light affliction of Zebulon and Naphtali*, Isaiah ix. i, compared with the *total* darkening of their typical Heavens, when passing away, (with the typical dispensation of Moses) under the judgment predicted over the Anti-christian Jewish Church of the Apostolic age? (Dan. xii. with Matt. xxiv.)

THE CURVES AND RADIATING HOUR-LINES OF THE GREEK-EGYPTIAN SUN-DIAL WITH STEPS.

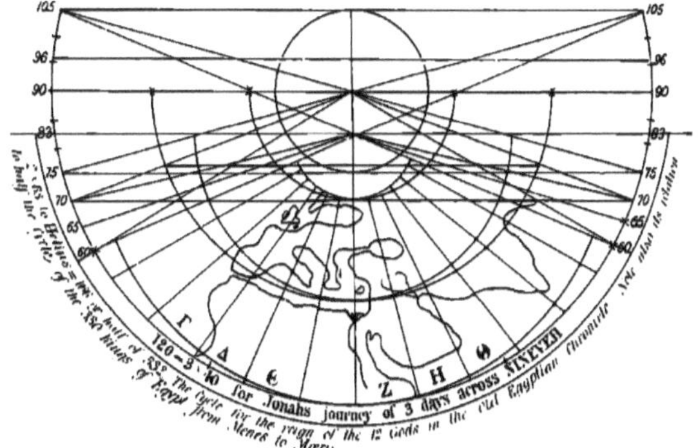

The Curves of the Greek-Egyptian Sun-Dial with Steps, applied to the construction of a similar Dial for Whitby. N. Lat. 54°.

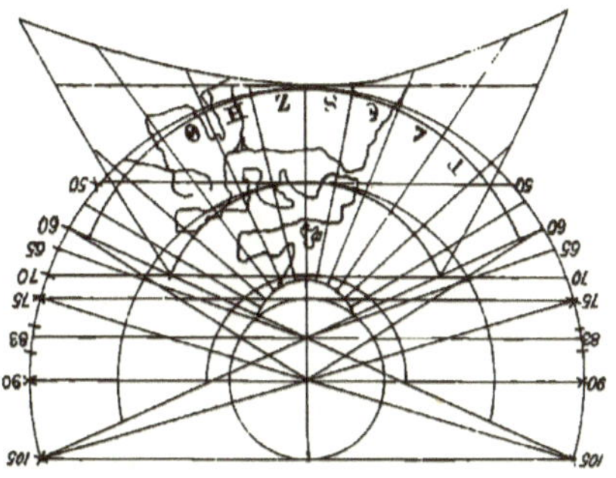

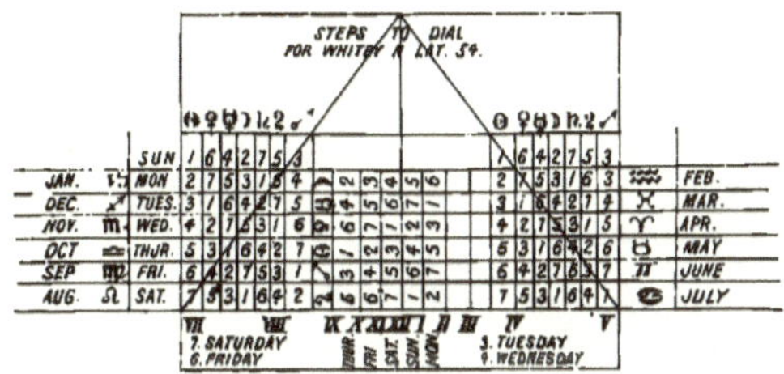

Signs of the Zodiac, arranged to the Analemma as on the Zodiac of Tentyra.

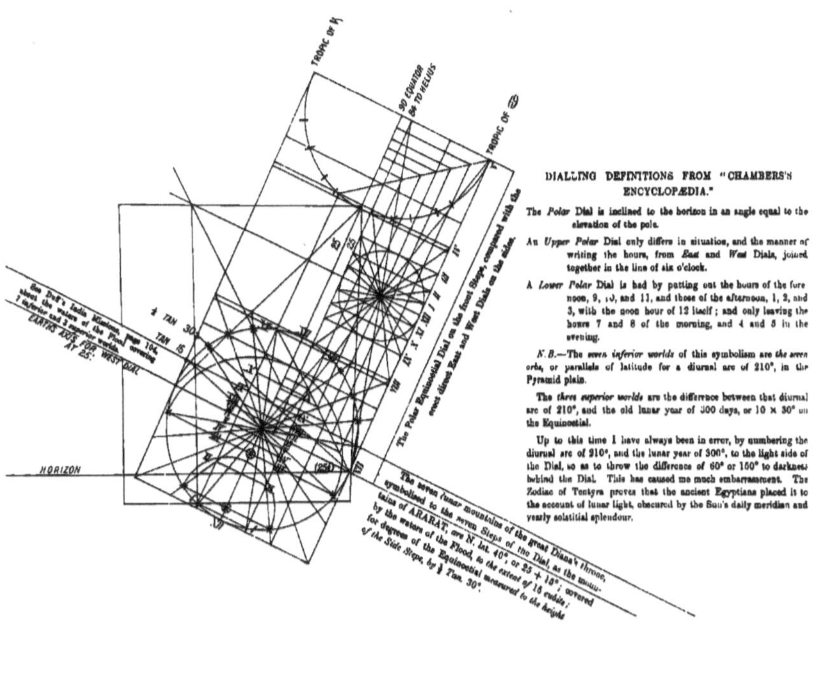

DIALLING DEFINITIONS FROM "CHAMBERS'S ENCYCLOPÆDIA."

The *Polar* Dial is inclined to the horizon in an angle equal to the elevation of the pole.

An *Upper Polar* Dial only differs in situation, and the manner of writing the hours, from *East* and *West* Dials, joined together in the line of six o'clock.

A *Lower Polar* Dial is had by putting out the hours of the fore noon, 9, 10, and 11, and those of the afternoon, 1, 2, and 3, with the noon hour of 12 itself; and only leaving the hours 7 and 8 of the morning, and 4 and 5 in the evening.

N.B.—The *seven inferior worlds* of this symbolism are *the seven orbs*, or parallels of latitude for a diurnal arc of 210°, in the Pyramid plain.

The *three superior worlds* are the difference between that diurnal arc of 210°, and the old lunar year of 300 days, or 10 × 30° on the Equinoctial.

Up to this time I have always been in error, by numbering the diurnal arc of 210°, and the lunar year of 300°, to the light side of the Dial, so as to throw the difference of 60° or 150° to darkness behind the Dial. This has caused me much embarrassment. The Zodiac of Tentyra proves that the ancient Egyptians placed it to the account of lunar light, obscured by the Sun's daily meridian and yearly solstitial splendour.

S. GEORGE FROM A MS. IN THE BODLEIAN LIBRARY.

FROM BRINSOP CHURCH, HEREFORDSHIRE.

PUBLISHED AS AN ILLUSTRATION IN THE CALENDARS OF THE ANGLICAN CHURCH, BY JOHN HENRY PARKER, OXFORD AND LONDON, A.D. 1851.

ENOCH'S SIX EASTERN AND SIX WESTERN GATES OF HEAVEN, divided into two Cycles of Seven and two of Five, by counting the Fifth and Seventh twice.

Thus the Jews divided their year of 12 months into two typical Cycles of 5 and two of 7 months.

Compare the MITHRAIC Symbolism of the *Seven* against THEBES.

The Eastern Signs of the Zodiac to the morning hours of a Quadrant Dial, and to the Lunar Calendarium of 5 days. This chronicles the Descent of the great Diana of the Ephesians from Jupiter.		Mon.	Sun.	Sat.	Fri.	Thur.				Theban Chiefs to Enoch's Eastern gates of Heaven.	Saturn here dethroned by the fall between the semicircular dial, and the top step.			Argive Chiefs to Enoch's Western gates of Heaven.			♄	7 Sat.	1 Sun.	2 Mon	*3 Tue.	4 Wed	☿	Western Signs of the Zodiac to the afternoon hours of a Quadrant Dial, and to the Lunar Calendarium of 5 days. This chronicles the Descent of the great Ephesian Diana from Jupiter, and illustrates the meaning of "a Jove principium."
	☽	2	1	7	6	5	♃	Jup.	♑ Jan.	Lasthenes	1	1	Amphiaraus	Feb.	♒	☽	2	3	4	5	6	♀	
	♄	7	6	5	4	3	♂	Mars	♐ Dec.	Hyperbius	2	2	Parthenopæus	Mar.	♓	☿	4	5	6	7	1	☉	
	♃	5	4	3	2	1	☉	Sol.	♏ Nov.	Megareus	3	3	Eteoclus	April	♈	♀	6	7	1	2	3	♂	
	♂	3	2	1	7	6	♀	Ve.	♎ Oct.	Polyphontes	4	4	Capaneus	May	♉	☉	1	2	3	4	5	♃	
	☉	1	7	6	5	4	☿	Mer.	♍ Sept.	Menalippus	5	5	Tydeus	June	♊	♂	3	4	5	6	7	♄	
	♀	8	8	4	3	2	☽	Lun.	♌ Aug.	Polynices†	6	6	Eteocles†	July	♋	♃	5	6	7	1	2	☽	
	☿	4 Wed	*3 Tue.	2 Mon	1 Sun.	7 Sat.	♄	Sat. goes out to hour of xii., on the seventh step, for return of the Cycle from Monday to Friday, Eastward.												3*			
		vii	viii	ix	x	xi											Thur. i	Fri. ii	Sat. iii	Sun. iv	Mon. v		

* For the seventh step numbered to Saturn as going out‡—or rather as numbered partially to the old & new day of the week, *i.e.*, on the Calendarium for the Cycle of 5 days beginning from Thursday; whilst Sunday is the day which goes out on the week of 7 days beginning from Friday to Venus when reduced to a Calendarium for 6 days—reckoned tropically to ascending and descending light—on the Analemma for the Sun's two half yearly circuits of six months from Tropic to Tropic. As the Planetary symbols can only be read intelligibly on the Calendarium from left to right, whilst the Morning and Evening hours stand inversely to one another on a Quadrant Dial, we seem to trace in the mode of comparing the Planetary symbols with these hours, the origin of that ancient mode of writing called Βουστροφηδὸν (ploughing fashion, as turning from left to right and from right to left, alternately,) by the Greeks.

† † Like that of the Roman gladiators—termed MERIDIANI—the hand to hand contest between the two brothers, *in the Seven against Thebes*, viz., that of Eteocles, "the glory of the year," and senior by birthright, (as in the cases of Cain, Esau, and Manasseh, with Abel, Jacob, and Ephraim, for their younger brothers,) against Polynices, the *oft victorious*, but regarded by his brother *as the contentious*, is given *Eastward and Westward to the Meridian hour*, as that of the Sun's *sixth* gate in the astronomy of Enoch.

The others are arranged in two companies of *five*, viz., Westerns against Easterns, *in parallel rows*, as Enoch placed his *other ten astronomical gates of heaven, in two parallel rows of five, for a Tropical reckoning*, like that of the ancient oriental writing called, by the Greeks, "Ploughing fashion."

‡ Whether the *nearly* obliterated figure on the Calendarium of the Ham Dial should be 7 or 3, I cannot say with precision. But if Saturn (♄) represents the *third* hour of Wednesday at the top of the first column, then 1 for Sunday as the *first* day in the fourth column, would represent the third hour of Thursday as dedicated to Jupiter. The second hour, therefore, should be dedicated to *Mars, for Tuesday, the third in our week.* Hence, I think, there is sufficient reason to place the figure 3, instead of 7, immediately before 1, as numbered to the fourth day of the week beginning from Thursday. This verifies the Hindu symbolism for Ganesha, or Saturn, at the right hand of Durga, and Katikeya (as the Mars of the Greeks) on her left hand.—N.B. The Days of the Week are numbered to Monthly Cycles of 6 × 5 = 30, or 7 × 5 = 35, for 4 × 9 = 36 days; to two Egyptian hours of Pheron, the Son of Sesostris. But the Planetary hours are numbered to Planetary Cycles of 5 days each, seemingly to compare the old Chaldean month of 30 days with the old Hindu day of 30 hours, referred to by COLEBROOKE in his *Essays on the Religion and Philosophy of the Hindus.*

See Rev. ix. 15, for the ancient Oriental mode of *typically* computing *hours, days*, and *months*, and years, in common Cycles, whether of 5, 7, 6, 9, or 10 days; or under any other variation in their subdivisions of typical time.

This brings me to a new and possibly conclusive view on the subject. When preparing for my ministerial duties of Sunday, May 5th, 1867, Numbers xxiii., xxiv., being the first Lesson appointed for the Morning Service. This brought me to consider Balaam's typical sacrifice of *Seven Bullocks* and *Seven Rams*, in a light which had never previously occurred to me, viz., that of Enoch's two Lunar Circuits of *seven* and *two* of eight days in each of his Equinoctial lunations. The result was that I found the Equinoctial points, on the Egyptian Zodiac of Tentyra, placed between Aries (♈) and Taurus (♉). On naming this to my young mathematical friend, JOHN D. SMALES, of Esk Terrace, he said Did you ever compare the Roman Calendarium? My reply was, No; but it was stupid of me to have omitted; from the meaning of the old Etruscan word *iduare*, to divide; whence the derivation of the word *Ides* in the dividing of lunar and typical time.

When alone, I turned to the subject, and the result has been marvellous to myself. For it proves *clearly* and *fully* why Thursday was numbered the *second* day of the week on one Hindu Zodiac, whilst on the other it is accounted the fifth day, as by ourselves. The same mode of explanation is equally applicable to the other days of the week as differently numbered on the two Hindu Zodiacs. The law of the variation is this. As Enoch numbered two lunar circuits of *seven* and two of *eight* days to the month of 30 days, so the Romans reckoned two Cycles of Jupiter, or Cycles of 5 days, and two weeks of 9 days (query, *for the* 18 *Ethiopians of Herodotus)*; or two of 7, and two of 8, days, *for half a month* to the semi-equinoctial of 180° degrees on the Circle numbered as days, to half the old Solar year of the Chaldeans.

The details of this Calendarium, when illustrated from the Egyptian Zodiac of Tentyra, will stand thus,—

Five days for the relation of the Calends to the Nones, as 5th day in the week of 9 days, compared with that of 7 days; reckoned to Ascending light, Westward going North by the Dragon's head.

Ascending Node	Descending Node	Thursday to Jupiter for the Ides	Monday to June for the Calends	Mars Tuesday	Mercury Wednesday
4	3	2	2	3	4
♌	♍	♎	♏	♐	♑
		I Central Sun			
♋	♊	♉	♈	♓	♒
5	6 9 6	7 8 7	8 7 7	9 6 8	5
Mercury Wednesday	Mars Tuesday	Moon Monday	Saturn Saturday	Venus Friday	Jupiter Thursday

Five days for the relation of the Calends to the Nones, as the 5th day in the week of 9 days, compared with that of 7 days; reckoned to Descending light, Eastward going South by the Dragon's tail.

The Nones (or *ninth* day before the Ides, in the dividing of typical time) were reckoned from the *seventh* day of the month, in *March, May, July,* and *October*, but in all the other months they were reckoned from the 5th. This symbolism compares the Ancient Oriental day of 30 hours with the month of 30 days; for seven typical months compared with the seven typical days of Gen. i.; and with Enoch's lunar circuit of seven days, in his two Equinoctial lunations of 30 days, divided to Ascending and Descending light between the Sun's *third* and *fourth* gates.

Note the typical situation appointed for the *three cities of refuge*, Deut. iv. 41, "*On this side* the Jordan toward the sunrising;" viz., "Bezer in the wilderness," &c., in its relation to the direction which Balak, King of Moab, brought Balaam, "*from* Aram, *out of the mountains of the east*, saying, Come, curse me Jacob, and come, defy Israel."

It also throws a clear light upon a statement made by the author of the *Key to the Chronology of the Hindus*, vol. ii. pp. 376-8, that the *seventh* day of the week was dedicated to JUPITER, saying, "those Indians who make Saturday the *seventh* day, invariably dedicate it to Jupiter." He adds,—"Mythologists frequently mistake this dedication of the planets, annexing a particular day of the week to each; without regarding the day on which the week commenced. Whereas the planet depends on the number of days from the first. For example: the Sittaanders commencing the week from Sunday, that day is sacred to Venus, [query, the Sun? as first in their account;] Friday to Mercury; and Saturday to Jupiter; because they are the *first, sixth,* and *seventh* days of the week. For the same reason, the Fakeers who commence the week from Friday, dedicate that day, Wednesday, and Thursday, to Venus, Mercury, and Jupiter; as will more clearly appear from the following table:

SITTAANDERS.	FAKEERS.	Order of Planetary Dedications, (but possibly under limitation to the *week beginning from Friday.)*	
1st Sunday	1st Friday	1st Venus.	
2nd Monday	2nd Saturday	2nd Saturn.	Satyavatar.
3rd Tuesday	3rd Sunday	3rd Sun.	
4th Wednesday	4th Monday	4th Moon.	
5th Thursday	5th Tuesday	5th Mars.	
6th Friday	6th Wednesday	6th Mercury.	Buddha, an incarnation of Vishnu.
7th Saturday	7th Thursday	7th Jupiter."	

According, however, to BLUNDEVIL, The *seventh* day of the week would be dedicated to Jupiter, when the *first* was dedicated to *Venus;* but the *seventh* was dedicated to Saturn when the first was dedicated to the Sun. The planetary dedications of the remaining days, varied according *to the day on which the beginning of their week was dedicated to the beginning of typical time*, whether dating the first day from the Winter Tropic, for the beginning of typical time on an East and West Dial, or from the 3rd day of Creation, as given to the Moon, whilst the fourth was given to the Sun when symbolizing *descending light to the Moon* (for the ancient beginning of typical time as symbolized to *the birth of Night, before that of Day,) but ascending light to the Sun's diurnal arc*, beginning—like *the typical year* of Mosaic institution—*from the Sun's fourth gate in the astronomy of Enoch.*

Possibly the Calendarium of the ancient Romans will afford another illustration. For whilst they dedicated the Calends, or first of the month, to Juno, they dedicate the Ides, or dividing of *monthly* or *lunar* typical time to *Jupiter*. Now the division of the *week* of nine days into two half Cycles of five days was as that of their half month divided into two lunar circuits of *seven* days. Hence the *Nones* (which represented the dividing of *weekly* lunar time) were sometimes numbered as the *fifth*, at others as the *seventh* from the Calends. Thus in a week of nine days, beginning from the Sun and ending with the Moon, reckoning from Sunday to Monday a week of 9 days, *Thursday* as *fifth* day will be in the dividing of time.

But in a half month of 14 days, beginning from Friday dedicated to Venus, Thursday will be both the *seventh* and the first of a week of *seven days ending with Wednesday*, or of *nine days ending with Friday*, for the typical relation of the Calends to the Ides.

On comparing the Cycle of 5 with the old week of 9 days, the ancient Orientals divided the Circle of the Equinoctial into 30 equal parts, to represent a day and night of 30 hours, compared with the month of 30 days, and divided into two Half Cycles of 15, each typically numbered to six signs of the Zodiac. Thus they divided their days, like their lunations, into *three*, as well as four, parts.

The Cycle of 9 they formed out of two Cycles of five, by counting the *fifth* day as fifth of both Cycles. Hence they added 9 to 5 for 2 x 7 = 14, to represent the *bright fortnight* of the sun's northern path. But Enoch also reckoned the increase of Lunar light *by three Quintuples of days, and its decrease likewise.*

The first of the month they called the *new* and *old* day, as divided into two half days: even as they divided the month into two Half Cycles. This is the explanation of Enoch, lxxii. 6—10, though I have hitherto but very imperfectly read the meaning of that passage already quoted.

This beginning and ending of lunar typical time they numbered to the sun's *sixth* gate, or *to the north ecliptic*, given to the West Horizon* on the hollow semicircular form of their East and West Dialling. They also symbolized the close of the Diurnal Arc eastward to the south ecliptic for the place of the full moon in the dividing of time equinoctially between day and night. This they thus did in two parallel Cycles of 12 hours, compared with two parallel half months of 15 days. These the Egyptians numbered to HORUS, and the 15 generations of the *Cynic* Circle so called (from the *dog-star*, at the Heliacal rising of which it commenced).† The Hindus called it *a Parouran* or half month.‡ Note, in further illustration of this, the Mithraic image of Osiris, *with his feet and toes of iron and potter's clay, turned towards the north* e. g., *the north ecliptic given to the West Horizon, as the place of the Holy of Holies, in the Jewish typical sanctuary.*

The imagery thus viewed makes the reference to "the ships of Chittim" in Baalam's typical prophecy, far more intelligible than, as generally interpreted with vagueness, "ships from the West," though in point of historical fact it makes no difference, for the prophecy was fulfilled by Greeks and Romans against Jerusalem in "the latter days" of the Mosaic or typical dispensation.

But the accuracy of the interpretation here contended for *is of importance* to substantiate the meaning I have elsewhere set upon Rev. ix. 15—that the warlike spirit of the world divided against itself to mutual slaughter (as of old under conflicting impulses of human ambition, traditionally cherished) should continue its desolations, *until the new order of things, predicted as the object of Messiah's manifestation in the flesh, should be realized with spiritual and truthful effect for the happiness of man.* Hence the Chronology is typical, and figurative, as applied by Virgil to the peaceful reign of Augustus *inaugurating a new state of things, as by the dawn of a new day.*

"Jam novus, e Cœlo, Sæclorum nascitur ordo."

For Gesenius, under the word Chittim, says, "The singular does not occur in the Old Testament, but is found in a bilingual inscription at Athens, where the proper name of a man of Citium, buried at Athens, is written in Greek, "*Noumenios Citieus*," and in Phœnician letters, *Esh-Citti*, as the same with "Ben-Hodesh"—(*son of the new moon*) "a man of Citium." The Generic term means *smiters*—warriors.

---

* Compare Enoch's North Sea *and Cavity of the North* with the Dialling reference to the Great Western Sea, as that of the Pontus Euxinus to the Mediterranean in the expedition of the Argonauts.

† Hence the THOTH was dedicated to ANUBIS, or the Egyptian Hermes, symbolised with a dog's head. HORUS designates the Cycle as originally that of the Equinoctial divided to 24 hours of 15° or 60 minutes to an hour. When limited to the Lunar year of 300, it substituted two hour Cycles of 10 × 15° for two of 12 × 12° — 144°. Their reign of 143 years marks a double reference to the meaning of HORUS, *a Season*; for it adds the Quadrant reign of HELIUS, or 83, to the old Solar Cycle of 360.

‡ In Manetho's List of the Cynic Circle 15 names are mentioned. In the Key to the Chronology of the Hindus, the two Parouvans, or half months of 15 days, are not numbered to 30 according to the days; but to 24, as if for a division of the Equinoctial to an hour Circle of 24 × 15°. Hence we seem to trace from this remote antiquity a mode of converting two typical, or Planetary Cycles of 12 hours, into two of 14 or 15, by arranging them in parallel rows, so that the 3rd or 4th hour in the Lunar Cycle of 12 for night should represent the first hour in the Solar Cycle of 12 for day, as in Blundevil's Planetary Calendarium for our week of seven days, beginning from SUNDAY. This explains the contrast in Gen. i., between the calling of light out of darkness on the first day of creation; but not appointing the sun, and moon, and stars, *typically*, for signs and for seasons, for days and for years, until the *fourth day*. Also, the numbering of the *third* and *fourth* days to the nodes in the Cycle beginning from JUPITER.

The HINDU MONTHS of the year numbered to the half-weekly Lunar Calendarium of 5 days to illustrate what they meant by the light and dark fortnights of the month *Magha* for the beginning of their year from the Sun's entrance into Capricorn; whilst, like the Egyptians, dating the Thoth of their Lustrum, (viz., of their five years Cycle, which formed *the great* SOTHIAC YEAR of the Egyptians), from the Full Moon in Capricorn; as from the Solstitial dividing of Lunar typical time.

This symbolism gives the Central Sun to the Equinoctial points as going forth from that centre Northwards for Ascending light, and Southwards for Descending light under limitation of a Quadrant measure of distance from either Tropic. This they crossed by the semi-circular measure of the two Parouvans; one symbolising the ascension of light to a half month of 15 days, for the bright fortnight of the Sun's Northern path, from the new Moon in the Sun's sixth gate to the full Moon in the Sun's first gate; the other called *the dark fortnight of the month Magha*, beginning in 1° ♑, and ending at the place of the Moon's change for the next month in 1° ♒. Thus the Hindu month Magha was divided to the Equinoctial as the Cynic Circle of the Egyptians to their Sothiac year divided into two half Cycles, by their Thoth to the full Moon in ♑, and by their Sothis to the place of the Moon's change *in the Sun's sixth gate, in the astronomy of Enoch*, crossed by the Moon's Quarterings at the Equinoxes.

This explains the arrangement of the signs on the Hindu Zodiac which glories *in its central mountain of gold*, as for the hours of an East and West Quadrant Dial, when Evening preceded Morning in their astronomical day beginning from XII at noonday.

The Equinoctial as divided to the Horizon by the Hindus, to represent a Four-square City of Light round their Central Sun, compared with Blundevil's Dragon symbolism.

This they divided to their old weekly Cycle of 8 days to 8 Lokapalas, or Regents of the Spheres. The four at the cardinal points were Indra, Yama, Varuna, and Soma. The names of the others are Kuvera, Lord of Wealth, and King of the Yakshas; Vivaswat, one, a Prajapati, or mind-born; another, one of 12 Aditya, sons of Kasyapa; another the Sun, as father of Vawaswata Manu. Agni, God of Fire; and Vayu, God of the Wind, and King of the Gandharbas; but I do not know where to place them to the intermediate points of the horizon.

Soma, or the New Moon, ruler of the planets to North Ecliptic, for the Heliacal rising of the Dog star in Cancer.

Nabhas	Sravana	♌	Aug.	July
Nabhasya	Bhadra	♍	Sept.	Aug.
Isha	Aswina	♎	Oct.	Sept.
Urja	Kartika	♏	Nov.	Oct.
Sahas	Agrahayana	♐	Dec.	Nov.
Sahashya	Pausha	♑	Jan.	Dec.

Varuna, King of the Waters, Westward, to the NORTH, but Ketuma, regent of the West. p. 153.

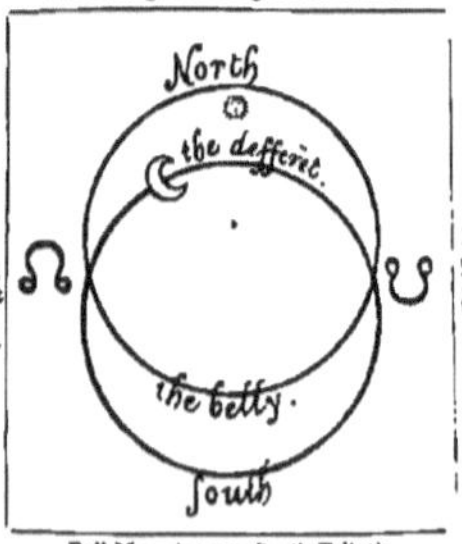

North

the defferet.

the belly.

South

Indra, King of the Gods, Eastward, to the North.

July	June	♋	Asharaha	Suchi.
June	May	♊	Tyeshtha	Sukra.
May	April	♉	Vaisackha	Madhava
April	Mar.	♈	Chaitra	Madhu
Mar.	Feb.	♓	Phalguna	Tapasya
Feb.	Jan.	♒	Magha*	Tapas

Full Moon in ♑ to South Ecliptic. Yama, King of the Pitris, or spirits of the departed, Southward. Add also, AGNI, a deity of fire. p. 83 & 153, n. 1.

The bright fortnight of Magha, for the Sun's *Northern* path from ♑ to ♋.

Moon's 3rd Quarter.

Query.—*Bright* when beginning from the full moon, but Dark when beginning from the new moon? or as *bright*, *Northwards*, to Summer, and *dark*, *Southward*, to Winter.

	♊ ♈ ♉	♓ ♒ ♑	
New Moon to Sun's *Sixth* gate.	Central the Quarter ☉ typical	Sun to ings of this lunation.	Full Moon to Sun's *First* gate.
	♋ ♌ ♍	♎ ♏ ♐	

The dark fortnight of SRAVANA, for the Sun's *Southern* path from ♋ to ♑.

The above typical Lunation of Magha, as reckoned *solstitially* from ♑ to ♋, and inversely for the halves of two lunations (when reckoning two months to a Solar season, and *three* seasons to a northern or southern declination, as in Wilson's Vishnu Purana, p. 223), is here crossed in like form, *equinoctially*, by those of the Aswins and Chaitra, or of Cartika and Vaisacha.‡

4. Pausha ♐ 5. ♑ Magha
3. Margasirsha ♏ 6. ♒ Phalguna
2. Cartika ♎ 7. ♓ Chaitra

The Bright fortnight or Sun's Northern path from Cartika in ♎ to Vaisacha in ♈.

The Dark fortnight, or Sun's Southern path from Aswina in ♍ to Chaitra in ♓, as from the new to the full Moon of the Autumnal Equinox.

1. Aswina ♍ 8. ♈ Vaisacha
12. Bhadra ♌ 9. ♉ Tyaishtha
11. Sravana ♋ 10. ♊ Ashlesha

Compare the old double month of the Solstitial Glory and the two Equinoctial Lunations of Enoch with the idea that Scorpio, like Cancer, had occupied an undue share of heaven, until Cæsar *held the balance of justice in Libra*—

Qua locus Erigonen inter Chelasque sequentis
Panditur: *ipse tibi jam brachia contrahit ardens*
Scorpios, et cæli justa plus parte reliquit.

—*Virg.*, Geor. i. 33.

The very ancient authority for this double series of two half months (Solstitial to Osiris, and Equinoctial to *Augustus* Cæsar; for Autumn as the intermediate season between Summer and Winter) is provable from the Vishnu Purana, as translated from the Sanscrit by Wilson.

Its importance also as a Chronological guide for safely interpreting *the typical language of ancient Jewish prophecy* is clear when reading the *otherwise, yet mystic*, language of Zech. xiv. 8–10. For when the typical months (dedicated by the ancient Hindus—Solstitially to Magha, and Equinoctially to the Aswins) intersect each other, for the *light and dark fortnight ascribed to each*, all is confused as to light and darkness, *humanly speaking*; as judged of by those ancient Oriental notions of *typical and prophetic time*, which were to *cease for ever in Messiah's day*. Rev. x. 6.

For then a NEW star (or that of *Bethlehem*) was substituted for the Remphan or FIVE-POINTED Dog Star of the idolators. Bethlehem means the House of Bread, as that of God's Providence over man in Christ, teaching him to understand that man liveth not by bread alone, *though associating* the mode in which He wills to be worshipped *with the sabbath sign of His own harvest mercies to man* in the Paradise of Oriental blessedness. That represented a latitude numbering 7 hours of ascending and 7 of descending light at the summer solstice. It also *made that perfect and equinoctial distinction between light and darkness*, which is referred to in Rev. xxii. 5 as marking an eternal purpose of God in Christ, for a spiritual distinction between good and evil in its issues, no less eternal and complete than that typically set before men in God's ordinances of day and night, respecting an eternal distinction between light and darkness in nature.

---

* The Month of Magha was dedicated to Ganesha by the Hindus, as January was to Janus, by the Romans. It formed the *Solar Solstitial Season* of 2 months typically reckoned as half months. The month of the ASWINS, formed similarly the *Solar Equinoctial Season* of two months each, divided into half months.

Thus the old Hindu notion of *two months to a Solar Season* is amply illustrated in the structure of the Calendarium on the Ram-shaped Dial for 5 × 6 = 30 days typically counted for 60. This Cycle they then multiplied by 5 (for each planetary hour was made to represent a Cycle of 5 days) to complete the Antediluvian Lunar year of 300 days, compared with the old Chaldean Solar year, or *Manwantara*, of 72 × 5 = 360 days of typical and prophetic time.

‡ Thus both Hindus and Egyptians typically divided the 12 months of the Solar year, into four quadrant measures of the Sun's apparent path through the 12 signs of the zodiac; and numbered each quadrant as a year. Thus the direction of sunrise and sunset would be *typically varied four times in the Lustrum, or great Sothiac year of the Egyptians*; and with reference to the lunation of 30 days when divided to the Equinoctial, into four quarters, as the priests told Herodotus. The 11,340 years of that reference being the days in 31½ old solar years of 360 days; for the days of the years of their great Lunar Cycle. The zodiacal belt of the MITHRAS D'ARLES is thus divided to four quadrants.

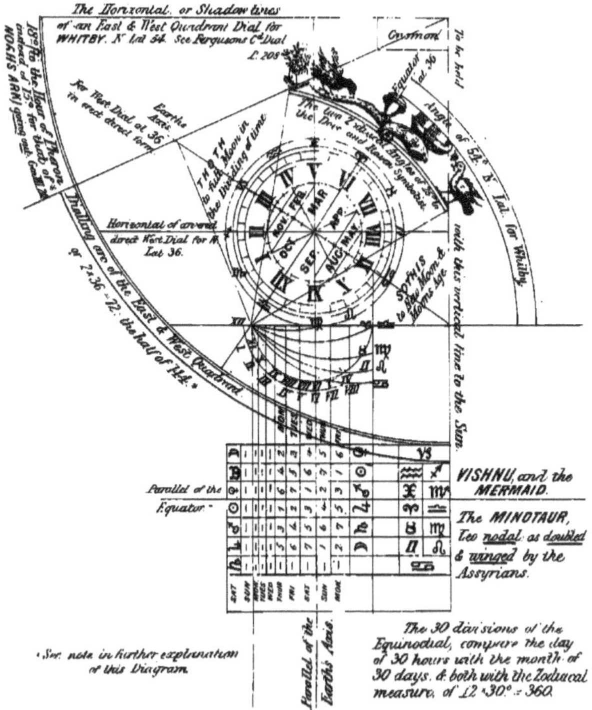

The Horizontal, or Shadow lines
of an East & West Quadrant Dial for
WHITBY. N. Lat 54. See Fergusons C^d. Dial
L. 208
Gnomon
To be held
Equator
Lat. 36
Angle of 54° N. Lat. for Whitby
with this vertical line to the Sun.
18° to the Hour of Pheron instead of 15° for the dial of NOAH'S ARK going out. Gen. VIII.
For West Dial at 36 in erect direct form
Earths Axis.
THOTH to fill Moon in the Dividing of time
The two Zodiacal Angles of 36° the Dove and Raven Symbolize
Horizontal of an erect direct West Dial for N. Lat. 36.
SOTHIS to give Moon & Moons Age
Dialling arc of the East & West Quadrant
or 2×36=72, the half of 144.*
NOV. FEB. MAR
OCT APR
SEP. AUG. MAY.
Parallel of the Equator
VISHNU, and the MERMAID.
The MINOTAUR, Leo nodal as doubled & winged by the Assyrians.
Parallel of the Earths Axis.
The 30 divisions of the Equinoctial, compare the day of 30 hours with the month of 30 days, & both with the Zodiacal measure of 12×30°=360.
* See note in further explanation of this Diagram.

HIEROGLYPHIC

FOR THE

NIGHT OF THE HALF MOON,

OVER THE SYMBOLISM OF THE ANCIENT ORIENTALS
FOR THE TREE OF LIFE IN THE MIDST
OF THE GARDEN OF EDEN.

The winged Disc, with another winged Symbolism of like character from the Gallery of Egyptian Antiquities, by Dr. S. Birch, of the British Museum.

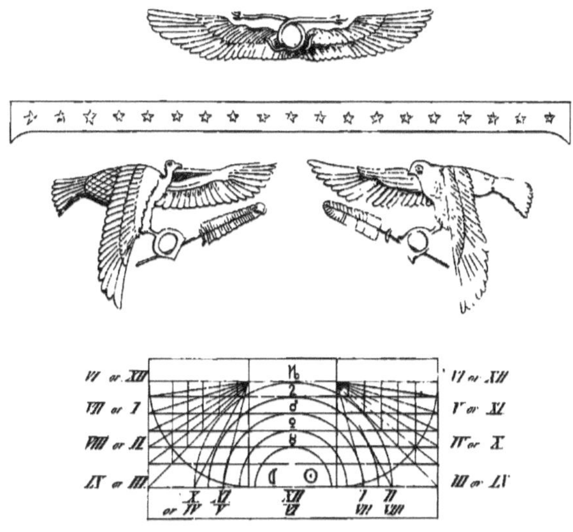

The Steps of the Greek Egyptian Dial divided to the Planetary Symbolism of Sylvanus Morgan. A.D. 1652, Also to a returning Cycle of 3 hours divided into half hours on the side Steps, the remaining hours being numbered to the front steps, as to the meridian of a Polar Dial or to the hour of VI: for the Evening & Morning of the primeval day, on the East & West Dialling of the Ancient Orientals. Gen I.

With the steps in this form compare the winged Disc of the Ancient Egyptian Hieroglyphics

A FRAGMENT OF AN OBELISK AT ROME

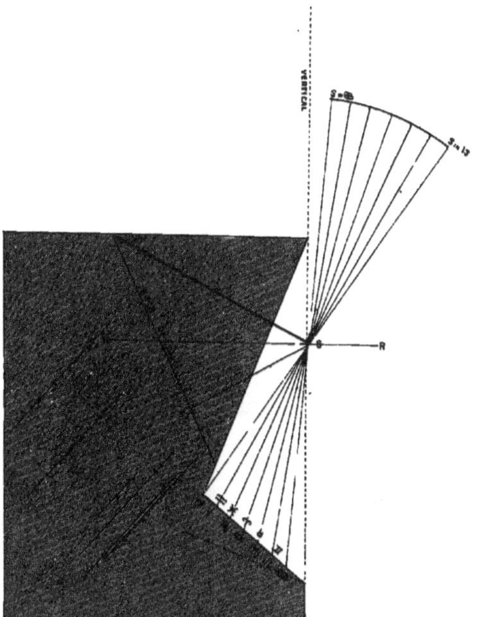

Delin. J. B. Smales, B.A. e Coll. Div. Joaham. A.D. 1869.

The dial appears to be a direct S. dial. If equinoctial angle be estimated as 25°
then for Lat. 30° when ☉ is in ♋ it is 5.° from vertical.

"The island of Elbo was 10.° on each side, or the difference between 709 & 720
half degrees."

ANCIENT AMERICAN CROSS

FROM THE RUINS OF PANLENQUE · CENTRAL AMERICA.

Sketched by J. Smales, Esq. from 'Stephens Central America'.

ANALYSIS OF THE PLANISPHERE TAKEN FROM THE TEMPLE OF TENTYRA.

"As a great sheet knit at the four corners, and let down to the earth."—Acts x. 10-17.

Symbolising the relation of the Circle to the Square; as "*the Island*" of the Mysteries, "*with a strong door and quadrilateral inclosure.*"

Compare Faber's *Origin of Idolatry*, vol. ii. p. 167, with the *four*-furrowed inclosure *sacred to Mars*, which Jason ploughed with fire-breathing bulls, and sowed with dragon's teeth.—*Apollonius Rhodius*, lib. iii. v. 1344 1358. The Cycle of the Solar year in its relation to their diurnal arc, on the east and west dialling of the ancients.

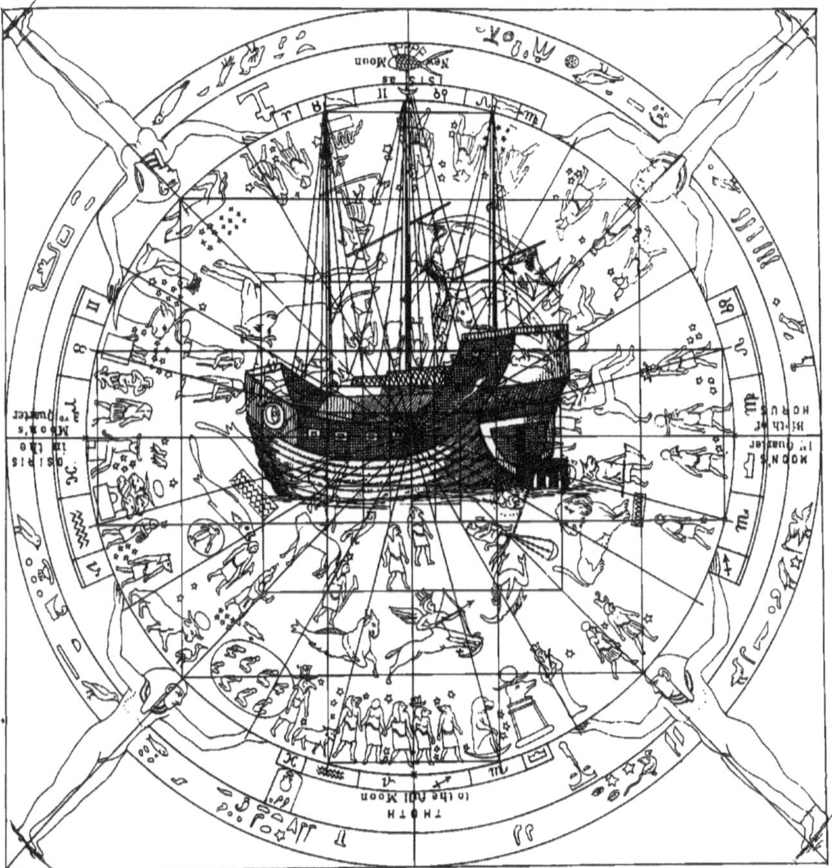

The EYE of PROVIDENCE on the equator of the Egyptian planisphere, divided to the hour lines of an east and west dial, compared with the six typical windows of a Chinese junk, having the Eye of Providence *on its prow*, and *the trident* of Neptune for its helm. Hence the "sacred ships" of the ancient Orientals, and the "ships of Tarshish" which Solomon sent to Ophir for gold, were probably of a like typical structure.

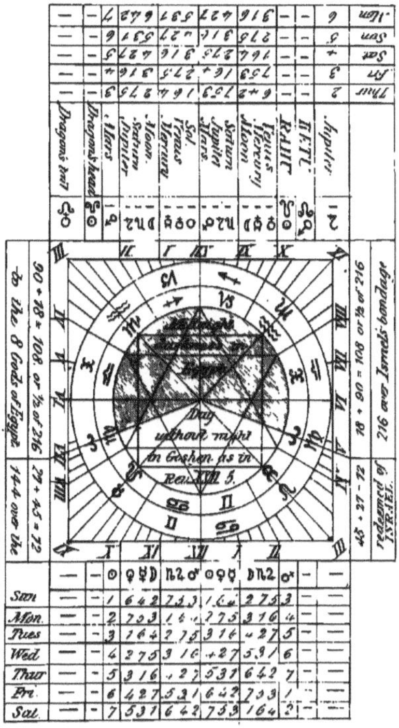

	—	—	☉	♀☿☽	♄♃♂	☉♀☿	☽♄♃	♂	—	—
Sun	—	—	1	6 4 2	7 5 3	1 6 4	2 7 5	3	—	—
Mon.	—	—	2	7 5 3	1 6 4	2 7 5	3 1 6	4	—	—
Tues	—	—	3	1 6 4	2 7 5	3 1 6	4 2 7	5	—	—
Wed	—	—	4	2 7 5	3 1 6	4 2 7	5 3 1	6	—	—
Thur	—	—	5	3 1 6	4 2 7	5 3 1	6 4 2	7	—	—
Fri.	—	—	6	4 2 7	5 3 1	6 4 2	7 5 3	1	—	—
Sat.	—	—	7	5 3 1	6 4 2	7 5 3	1 6 4	2	—	—

Day without night in Goshen as in Rev. XXII 5.

90 + 18 = 108, or ½ of 216 to the 8 Gods of Egypt

27 + 45 = 72 144 over the

18 + 90 = 108 or ½ of 216

216 are Israel's bondage

45 + 27 = 72

redeemed of ISRAEL.

	♃	☊ ♂	♌ ☉	♀☿☽	♄♃♂	☉♀☿	☽♄♃	♂	☊ ☉	☋ ♀
	Jupiter	ΠΕΤC	RAHC	Venus Mercury Moon	Saturn Jupiter Mars	Sol Venus Mercury	Moon Saturn Jupiter	Mars	Dragon's head	Dragon's tail
Thur	2	—	—	6 4 2	7 5 3	1 6 4	2 7 5	3	—	—
Fri	3	—	—	7 5 3	1 6 4	2 7 5	3 1 6	4	—	—
Sat	4	—	—	1 6 4	2 7 5	3 1 6	4 2 7	5	—	—
Sun	5	—	—	2 7 5	3 1 6	4 2 7	5 3 1	6	—	—
Mon	6	—	—	3 1 6	4 2 7	5 3 1	6 4 2	7	—	—

Piazzi Smyth's vertical section of the Great Pyramid, compared *on its east and west sides*, with the typical structure of the Greek-Egyptian Dial with Steps, considered as the hollow semicircle of the Babylonians, *inclined as an east and west Dial for the Pyramid plane in N. Lat.* 30°.

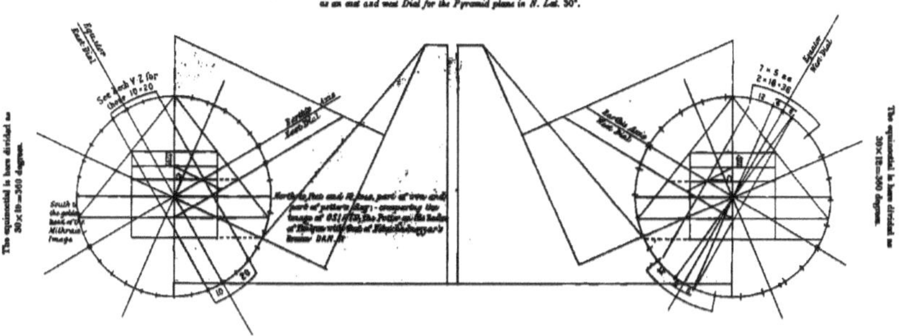

The INDUS and its tributaries to the PUNJAB, or region of *the 5 rivers, to the north-east*, on the inverted bell-shaped map of Hindostan.

But, on the maps of Egypt, the north is given eastward and westward, to the seven-mouthed DELTA of the Nile.

The north-east to MESOPOTAMIA, where Abram and Sarai first settled on migrating from Ur of the Chaldees.

This also was the abiding habitation of NAHOR and his descendants, when Abram, Sarai, and Lot crossed westward over the Euphrates, into the land of the Canaanite.

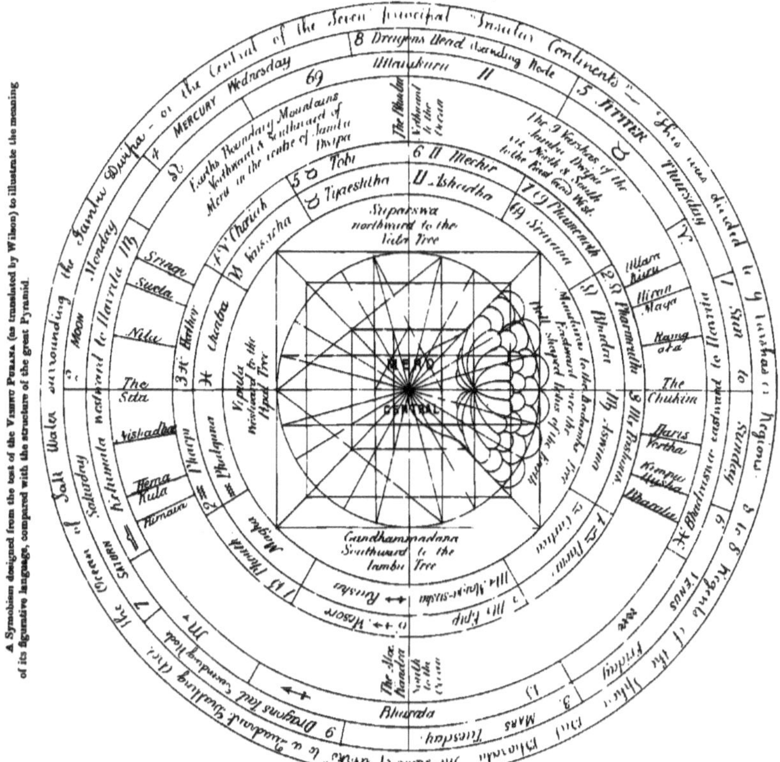

A Symbolism designed from the text of the VISHNU PURANA (as translated by Wilson) to illustrate the meaning of its figurative language, compared with the structure of the great Pyramid.

Piazzi Smyth's measurements for the typical chambers and galleries in the Great Pyramid, compared with the Hindu symbolism for the earth; as *a bell-shaped Lotus in its relation to Mount Meru*—considered as *an inverted cone*—on which was the abode of their heavenly gods.

Hence, seemingly, the compound symbolism of the Glasgow arms—received from St Mungo—viz.: 1. The bell; 2. The fish, for the sun in fishes at the beginning of their year; 3. The tree of life, under a different name to each quadrant of the equinoctial, even as the central river of Paradise flowed into the surrounding ocean of salt water from four heads.

The Delta of the Ganges with its seven mouths, symbolised to the south-east of Jambu Dwipa—viz., to Bharata Varsha.

But on the map of Egypt, the south-east is typically given to *the [illegible] mountain by the 12 [illegible]*; adjoining to Abyssinia, the Empire of Sheba, "Queen of the South" in Solomon's day.

The outer leaves of the Lotus are here numbered for a quadrant of 6 hours to the weeks of 6, 7, 8, and 9 days respectively.

East and West—Northward to the ascending node for Monday, Tuesday, and Wednesday.

To Horeb by the passage of the Red Sea at Baal Zephon.

To the midnight of Israel's Exodus from Memphis.

East and West—Southward to the descending node for Thursday, Friday, and Saturday.

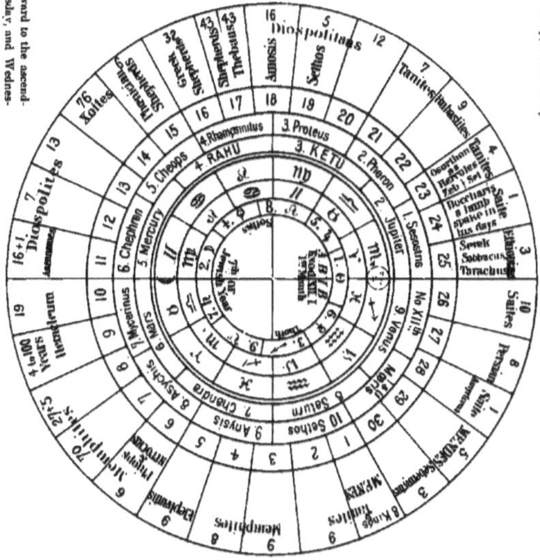

Top of the Symbolism to Sabacus and the Crocodile kings of Ethiopia.

N.B.—Menes was killed by a crocodile.

Manetho's XXX Dynasties of the Kings of Egypt, in its relation to their Cycle of XII Kings from Maris to Sethos; all of whom were also Priests of Vulcan.

The 50 sons of Egyptus to hours of East Dial.

The 50 daughters of Danaus to hours of West Dial.

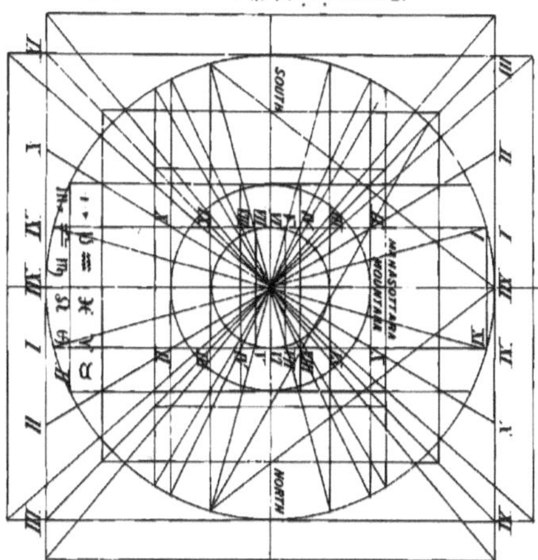

Twice 50 and twice 40 to twice 90°, for the diameter of the circle given to Hydra, dividing between the Dove and Raven symbolism, for ascending and descending light in the Noah's Ark lunar year of 300 days.

For the relation between Brahma's life of 100 years, and the diurnal arc of an east and west dial, substituting twice 50 for twice 45.

An attempt to verify Professor Piazzi Smyth's pyramid measurements from the symbolic geometry of the Vishnu Purana, and that of the promises made to Abraham and his seed, compared with the east and west typical dialling of the ancient orientals, as referred to in Zech. xiv. 4-10.

For our national emblem of the Lion and the Unicorn.

The Lion Westward to Jacob's right hand, as *given* to Ephraim.

The Unicorn Eastward to Joseph's left hand, as given to Manasseh. Hence, seemingly, the division of that tribe eastward and westward.

For our national emblem of the Lion and the Unicorn, to the hour-lines of an East and West Dial.

The Sun's South Declination to the Sun-Pharaohs of Egypt. For the 50 sons of Egyptus to the hours of an East Dial.

Hence their reckoning was eastward and westward to the *South in Capricorn;* as to Manasseh in Joseph's left hand towards Jacob's right hand.

The Sun's North Declination to the settlement of Israel in the land of Goshen, or the Delta of the Nile, northward in Egypt. For the typical relation of the 50 daughters of Danaus to the 50 sons of Egyptus; as of *Lunars* to *Solars.*

Hence their reckoning (for the hours of a West Dial) was eastward and westward to the *North in Leo;* as to Ephraim in Joseph's right hand towards Jacob's left.

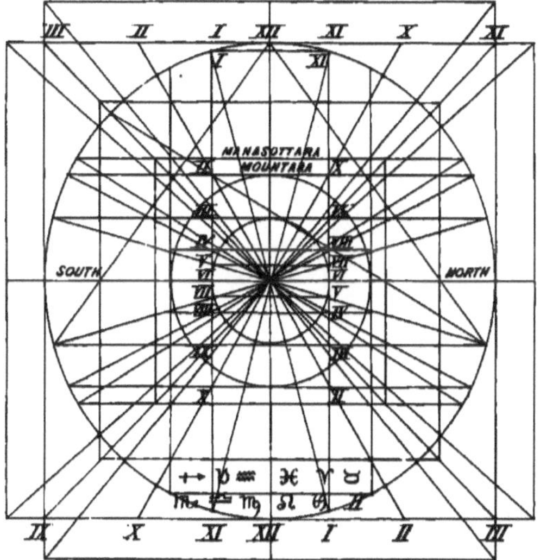

Twice 50 and twice 40 to twice 90°, for the diameter of the circle given to Hydra, dividing between the Dove and Raven symbolism, for ascending and descending light in the Noah's Ark lunar year of 300 days.

For the relation between Brahma's life of 100 years, and the diurnal arc of an east and west dial, substituting twice 50 for twice 45.

An attempt to verify Professor Piazzi Smyth's pyramid measurements from the symbolic geometry of the Vishnu Purans, and that of the promises made to Abraham and his seed, compared with the east and west typical dialling of the ancient orientals, as referred to in Zech. xiv. 4-10.

A CHINESE JUNK,

With the Eye of Providence on its prow, as of dialling relation to the typical structure of the ships of TARSHISH which SOLOMON sent to OPHIR for GOLD, thereby BAALISTICALLY corrupting the NOAH'S ARK dialling symbol of Jewish typical prophecy.

THE DIALLING CHARACTERISTICS OF NOAH'S ARK

VERIFIED ON THE TRIGON OF AN EAST AND WEST DIAL FOR THE TWO ZODIACAL ANGLES AT 25° INSTEAD OF $23\frac{1}{2}$°.

Turn over for comparison with the Chinese junk spanned by a dialling arc for 8 hours numbering 120°, as to Jonah's journey of 3 × 40, for 3 days, across the great city NINEVEH; and for the 120 talents of gold brought to King Solomon by SHEBA, Queen of the South (1 Kings x. 10).

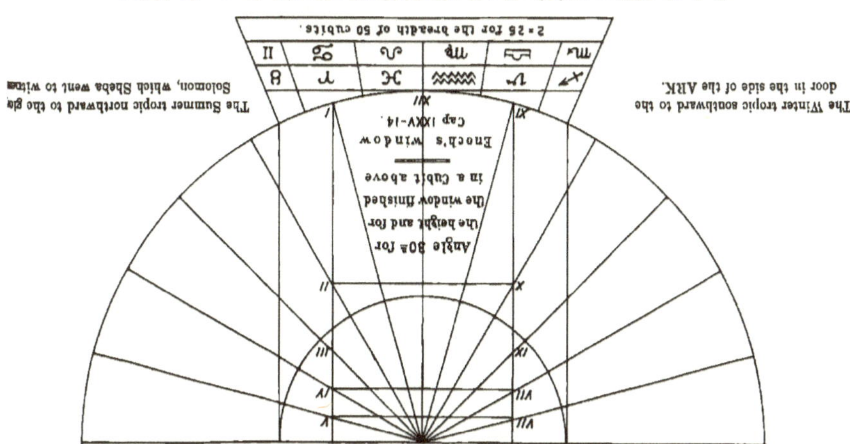

The length of 300 compared 12 × 25 as 10 × 30 with 12 × 30 as 10 × 36 for lunar months of 3 times 10 and 4 times 9 days, harmonised as yearly cycles of 10, compared with yearly cycles of 12 months for 100 years of 360 days equal 120 of 300 days, as the reference of Gen. vi. 3. This window, Enoch says, "at *a certain season* grows extremely hot."

The Old Saxon Dial at Kirkdale.

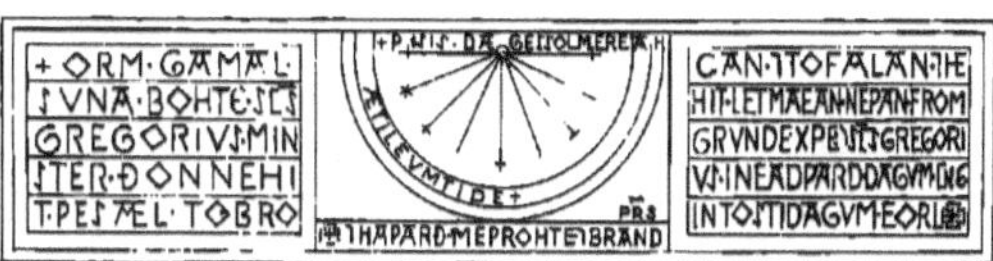

Dialling lines explanatory of the Kirkdale Dial —

These hour lines at 22½ degrees apart reckoned 90 minutes of time to 1½ Equinoctial hours

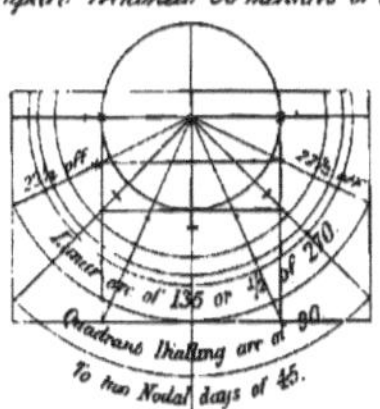

Compare the typical structure of the Ruswarp Dial combining a Dialling by the Analemma with the structure of the common Horizontal Dial.

The Old Saxon Dial at Edstone.

The hours number 80 minutes or 1 hour 20 minutes of Equinoctial time being hours of Enoch or 20.° to an hour

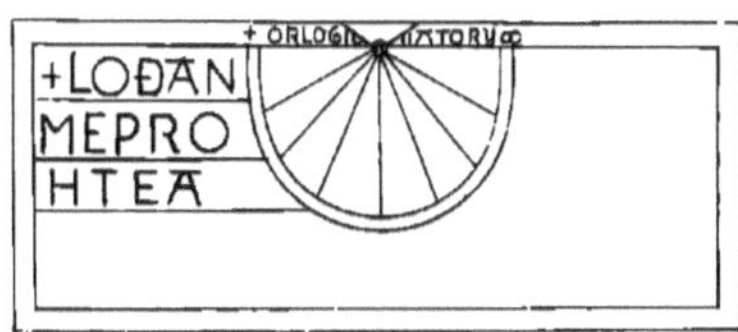

Dialling lines explanatory of the Edstone Dial.

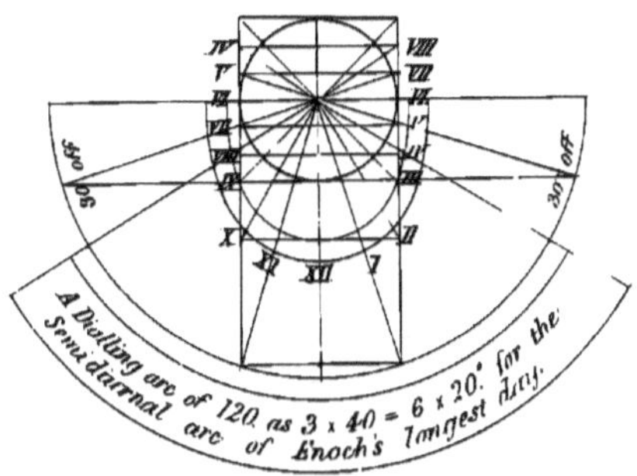

N.° 1. From the ordinary structure of an East & West Dial for hours of 60 minutes. —

An East. & West Dial for 12 hours of Enoch as hours of 80 minutes each, or 20°

No. 2. In explanation of the Edstone Dial compared with the seven central hours of the Greek Egyptian Dial: .

The Northern Palace of Sesostris, at the Pelusian Daphne viz. Northward to the Delta of the Nile, as set fire to by **TYPHON** or **APHOPHIS**, the Brother of Sesostris; and Dragon, - emblem of the Moons nodes. Herod II. Cap. 107. - Hence the titular designation for the Emperor of China; as Brother to the Sun and Moon. .

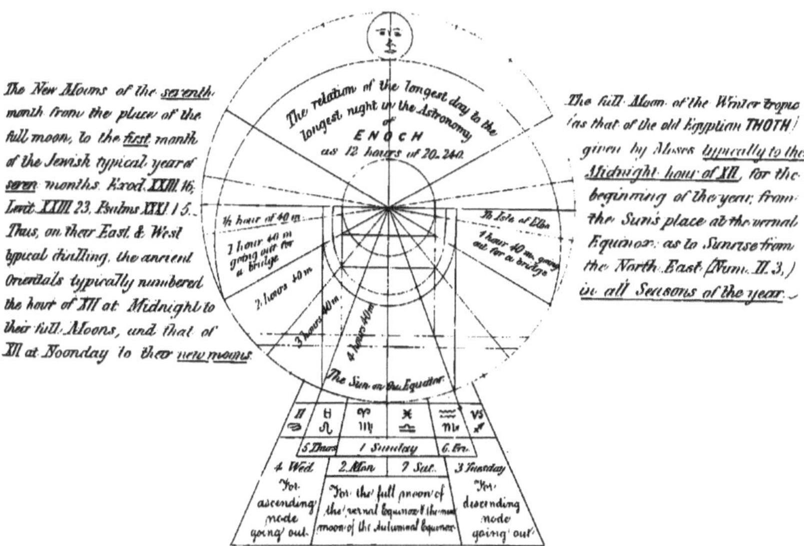
The New Moons of the seventh month from the place of the full moon, to the first month of the Jewish typical year of seven months. Exod. XXIII. 16; Levit. XXIII 23. Psalms XXXI 15. - Thus, on their East & West typical dialling, the ancient Orientals typically numbered the hour of XII at Midnight to their full Moons, and that of XII at Noonday to their new moons.
The relation of the longest day to the longest night in the Astronomy of ENOCH as 12 hours of 20 - 240
½ hour of 40 m
1 hour 40 m going out for a bridge
2 hours 40 m
3 hours 40 m
4 hours 40 m
To Isle of Elba
1 hour 40 m going out for a bridge
The Sun on the Equator
5 Thurs
1 Sunday
6 Fri
4 Wed.
2 Mon
7 Sat.
3 Tuesday
For ascending node going out
For the full moon of the vernal Equinox & the new moon of the Autumnal Equinox
For descending node going out
The full Moon of the Winter tropic (as that of the old Egyptian THOTH) given by Moses typically to the Midnight hour of XII, for the beginning of the year; from the Sun's place at the vernal Equinox: as to Sunrise from the North East (Num. II. 3,) in all Seasons of the year. -

Thus the two days numbered for the nodes (at 40° each) on the old Hindu Zodiac for the Baalistic week of 9 days, as rejected for a week of Seven, by the Jews & other Sabbatarians represent the two Children of Medea's Sacrifice. - Thus Sesostris and his Wife also sacrificed two of their Children to bridge a way over the long nocturnal arc of 240°. - (numbered as 20 days of lunar light monthly to "the man in the moon" Enoch XXVII. 21 - for the 20 cubits length of the flying roll, or "winged disc" of the Egyptians Zech. V. 2. - when the remaining 10 were numbered to a monthly obscuration of lunar light at the time of the new moon, compared with a daily obscuration by the Sun's meridian glory) to resume his daily reign of 120, when the nocturnal triumph of his brother Typhon extended over a nocturnal arc of 240°.

The 120° of this reference measured the 3 days of Jonah's journeying across the great City of **NINEVEH** (as 3 x 40) for the week of six days divided between ascending and descending light to the Sun and Moon on the Equator. See Isaiah XXX. 26. Zephes. IV. 9. 10: Malachi IV. 2.

Ferguson's construction of a Babylonian Dial for London, worked out, to show the relation of the Tropics to the Equator of the Dial plane.

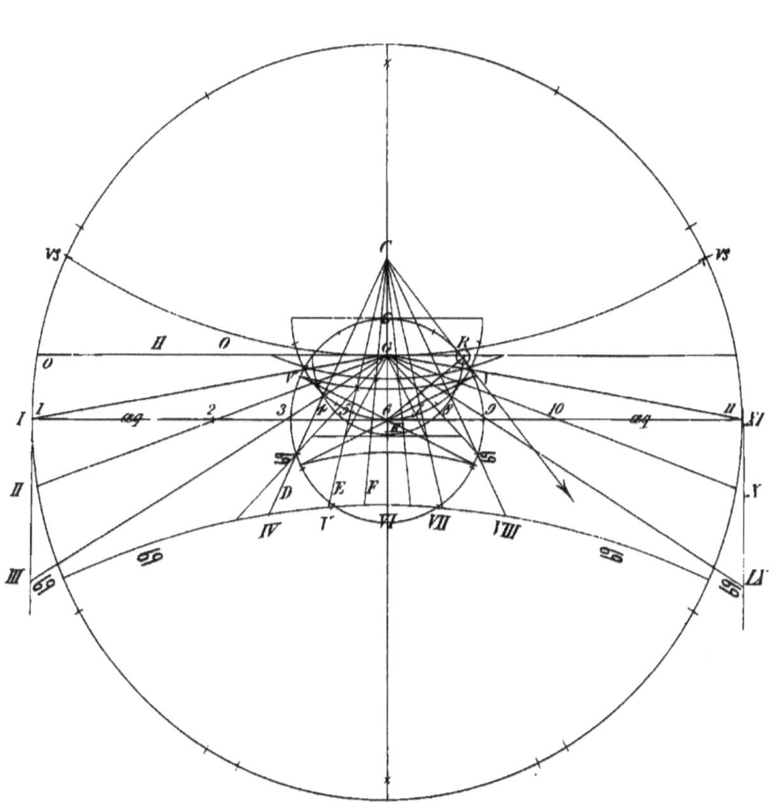

SHB's Beak.
For a Gnomon when Dialling
by <u>a point of Shadow.</u>

The 3 Cyclopes.—
For a Gnomon when Dialling
by <u>a point of Light,</u> from
Bedos de Celles.

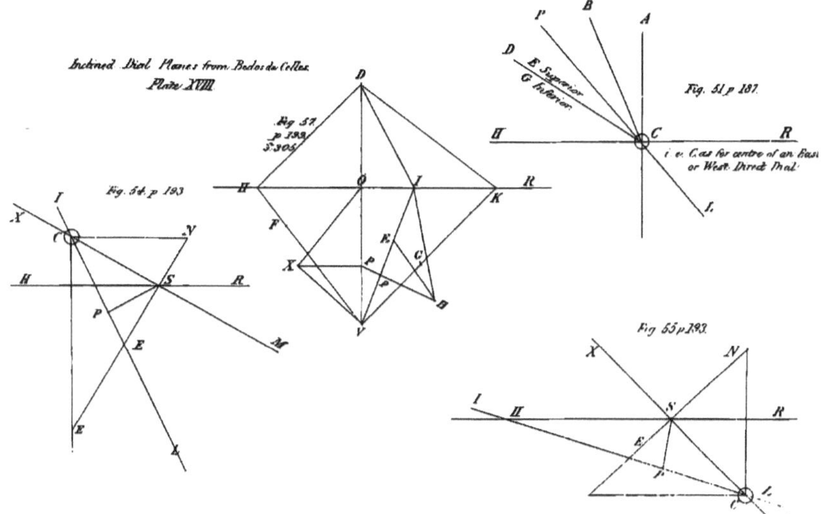
Inclined Dial Planes from Bedos de Celles.
Plate XVIII
Fig. 51 p 187.
P
B
A
D
E Superior
G Inferior
H
C
R
i. e. C as for centre of an East or West Direct Dial.
L
Fig 57. p 199. S. 305
D
H
O
I
R
K
F
E
G
X
P
P
B
V
Fig. 54. p 193
I
X
C
N
H
S
R
P
E
M
E
L
Fig 55 p 193.
X
N
I
H
S
R
E
P
C
L
M

Meridians _ from Bedos de Celles _ for marking the Sun's place in the Ecliptic, on Horizontal, South-vertical, and Declining Dial Planes.

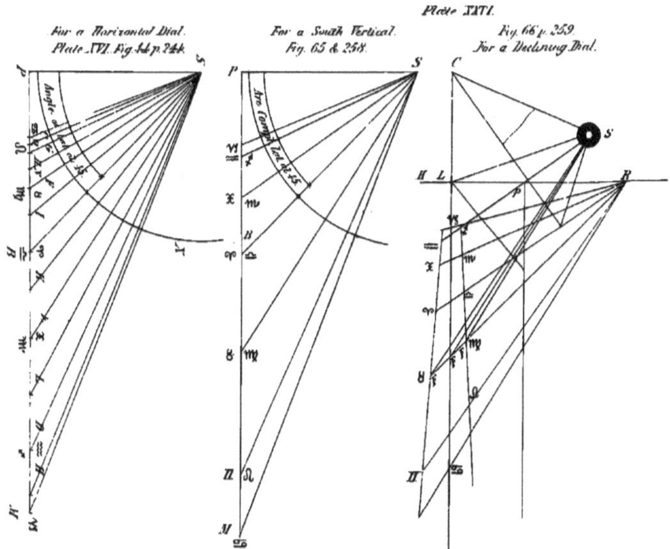

Fig. 1. The Fundamental Dialling Diagram of Sylvanus Morgan.— Fig. 2. His mode of making an erect Vertical Declining Dial.—I have here substituted a Declination of 35°30' for his of 45° and the Latitude of Whitby for that of London; nor have I given other hour lines than those the points of which are found on the Horizontal line. Fig. 3.—This Diagram for determining the relation between the Angle of Declination and that of the Co-Latitude.

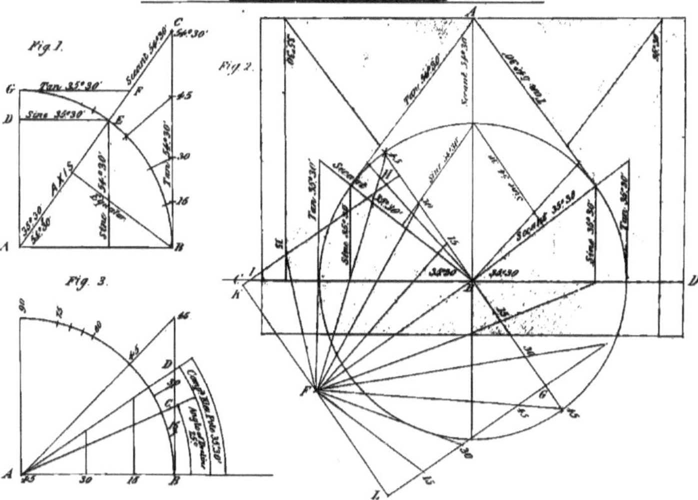

To keep the hour lines of a Declining Dial within a right angled parallelogram.

This Diagram is as that of Sylvanus Morgan merely substituting the Latitude of Whitby and a Declination of 25°, for his of 30°. His mode of finding the hour-lines is moreover verified by applying that of Bedos de Celles; for the span of the Equinoctial between the hours of VI & XII.

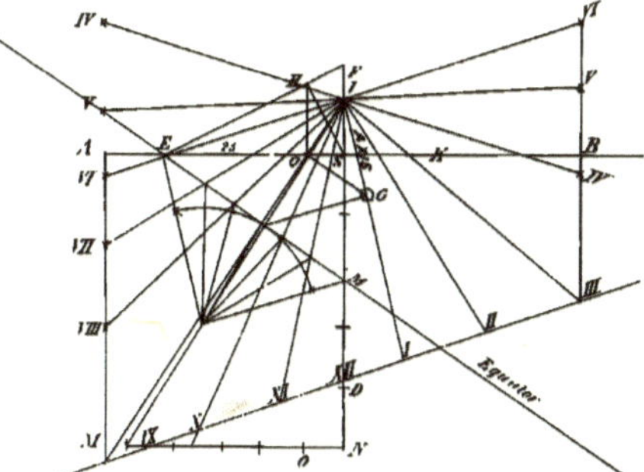

New Diagram

For the relation of the steps to the curves.

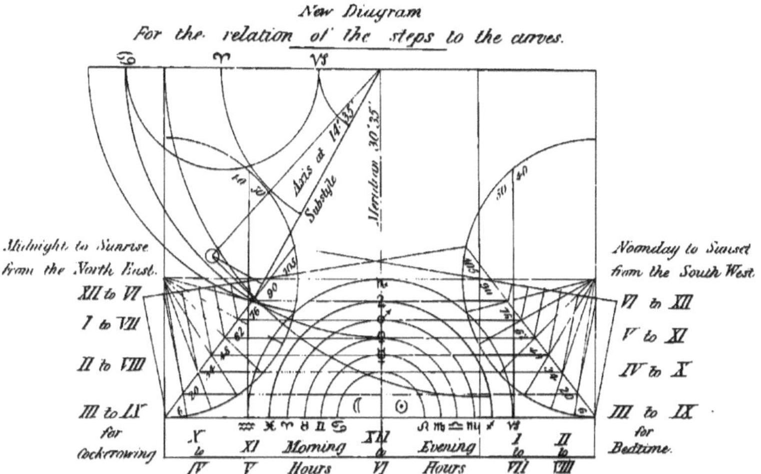

Noonday to the "Dividing of time" typically between East and West.

For the evening before morning of Gen. I. & Zech. XIV.

Illustrating Isaiah XXX. 26.

From the "Nychthemeron" of the Ancient Orientals. For that began their equinoctial night and day of 24 hours from Sunset to the Autumnal Equinox, whilst we begin our day and night of 24 hours from Sunrise to the Vernal Equinox: But, in Dialling, the Eastern Signs are numbered to the morning hours westward on the Horizon, from Sunrise to Noonday, and the Western Signs to the afternoon hours eastward on the Horizon, from Noonday to Evening. This will also explain Herod II. v 142, that (within their typical Quadrant Dialling for the Cycle of their new moon; as, I understand the interpretation by Mr E. Sang of Edinburgh) "The Sun had four times deviated from his ordinary course, having twice risen where he uniformly goes down, and twice gone down where he uniformly rises."

The steps of the Greek Egyptian Dial shewing how the Hour lines should be put to steps.

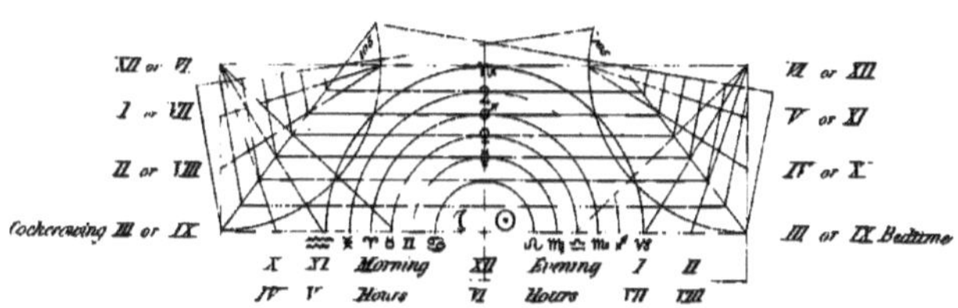

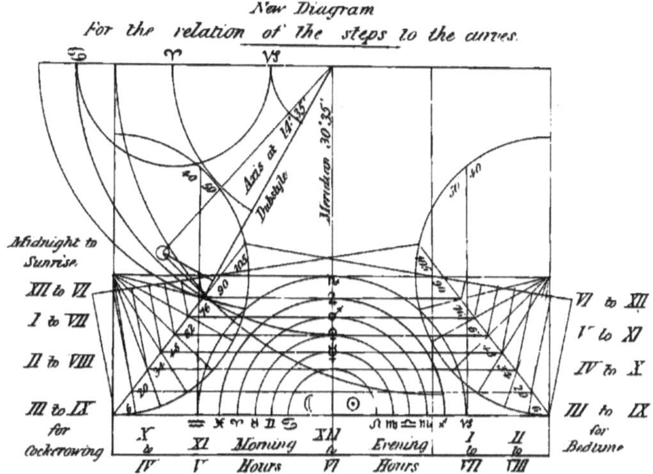

Noonday to Sunset.

For the evening before morning of Gen. I. & Zech. XIV.
and illustrating Isaiah XXX. 26.

Thus the Enoch's before morning for the beginning of typical time in the moon's Desending Node seems to have given the six closing hours of a West Dial. viz. from sunset to midnight typically to to suns dialling light between noonday to sunrise.

The Steps divided for a Semidiurnal Arc of 7 hours (as 7 x 15 105) for the longest day in S. Lat. 30. reduced to one of 6 hours, for a Quadrant Measure of the Sun's varying altitude throughout the year; compared with Enoch's Quadrant of 91 = 7 x 13°; for a weekly lunar circuit of seven days.

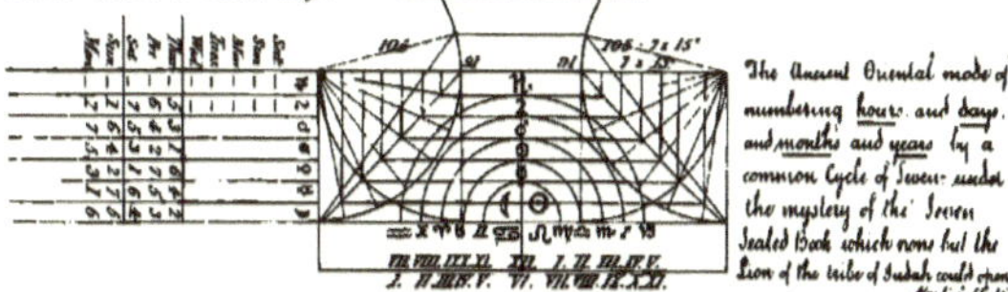

The Ancient Oriental mode of numbering hours and days, and months and years by a common Cycle of Seven under the mystery of the Seven Sealed Book which none but the Lion of the tribe of Judah could open.

N.B. This seems to me to explain the object of the fall between the Curved part and the Steps, as one with that for which the side Steps have an inclination of 15° above the angle of Latitude.

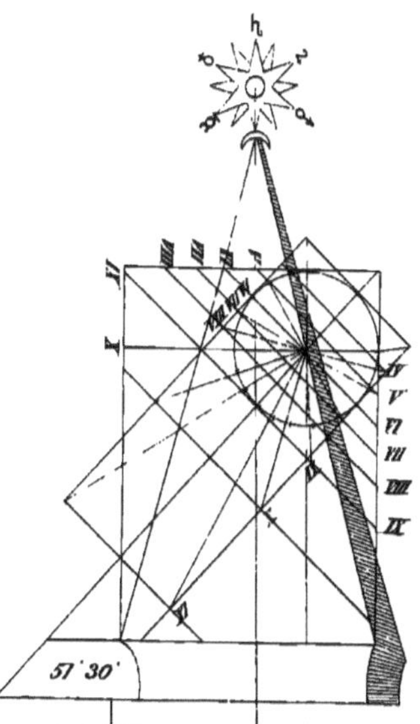

The Astronomical Pillar in the Court of Arts, by Sylvanus Morgan in its relation to the hour lines of an East Dial with the style's height over the hour of VI limited between the intersection of the Angular Incline and central line of sloping side by Earth's Axis. There is a similar column without the Dial; fronting the Museum at Arles. Though the hours are numbered as above for an East Dial; by Sylvanus Morgan, this side of the Pyramid, will only give the afternoon hours of a West Dial in the Sun as tried by myself in the Sun. For I know not how to present such a dial southward to the Sun; & therefore cannot conceive this to be the meaning of his words; "on the South side (viz. of this pyramidal pillar consecrated to art) — stood ASTRONOMIA, *respecting the Sun, & on the North side* GEOGRAPHIA, *respecting the Pole;" seeing that reference to the Pole is as necessary for Dialling as for Geography.—*

Our earthly Sphere:

the Seat of "Clementia" the "Wisdom" of Prov. VIII v.1 & 22. representing Wisdom, Mercy & Power, harmonized In the Works of GOD:-

HENCE.

The Anatomical Figure of Sylvanus Morgan for the Sun's yearly course in the ecliptic symbolised to a female figure sitting on the World: with the head to Aries the centre of figure to Leo & Virgo, or to Virgo between Leo & Libra with Pisces under her feet, for the intercalary months between the old Lunar year of 10 months, as that of the flood season compared with the Solar year of 12 months.

The signs of the Zodiac are here arranged for an East & West, or Quadrant Dial as on the Zodical belt of the **MITHRAS D'ARLES.**

This Symbolism shews the relation of **VISHNUS** fish Avatar to the old Myth of the **MERMAID.**

Some of the Welsh legends respecting their old Queen Helen & the boulders deposited by her, or by some giant of those days- in the rivers & on the hills, evidently have reference to the old heathen superstition respecting the image of Diana which fell down, from Jupiter Acts XIX. 35. to set heathen Philosophers thinking even as we are in debted to the fall of an apple for the philosophy of SIR ISAAC NEWTON...

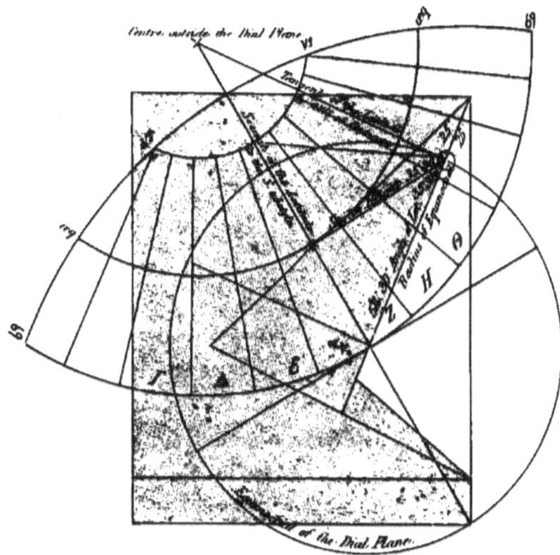

New imitation of the Greek Egyptian Dial, after the rule of Sylvanus Morgan, for an East & West Declining Dial in N. Lat 54°30'.~ The three curves of the hollow Semicircle (for the three stories of Noah's Ark) represent the Dialling of the ancient Babylonians for a day of 12 hours in all seasons of the year.~

An Upper Inclined East Dial adapted for Whitby N. Lat. 54°.30'. from Plate XX fig. 66 (see p. 82. of appendix to this tract) as a Declining South Vertical for Co-Latitude 35°.30'; illustrating the Typical structure of the Greek Egyptian Dial, with steps.

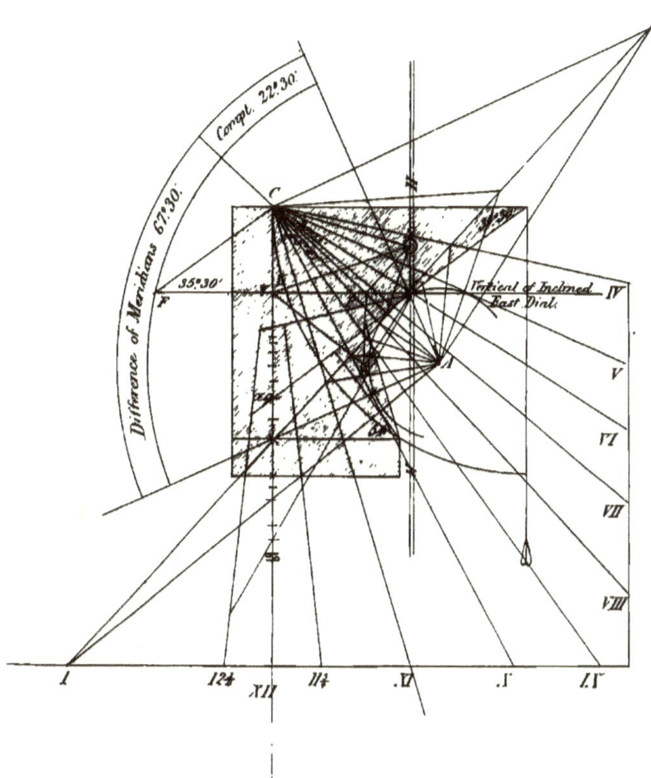

Application of the Greek Egyptian Dial for the Pyramid plain to the plane of the Goathland School Dial, as declining Westward from the South at an angle of 25°.

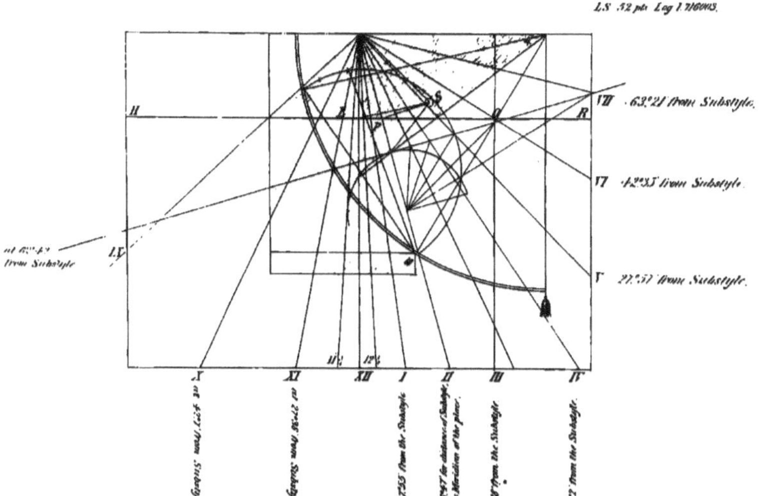

For a Meridian to The Goathland School Dial, Declining Westward — 25°
as on the West side of the Greek-Egyptian Dial, imitated for N. Lat. 54.

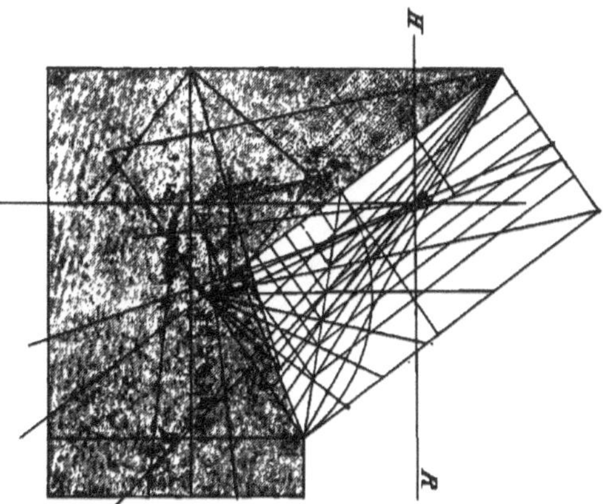

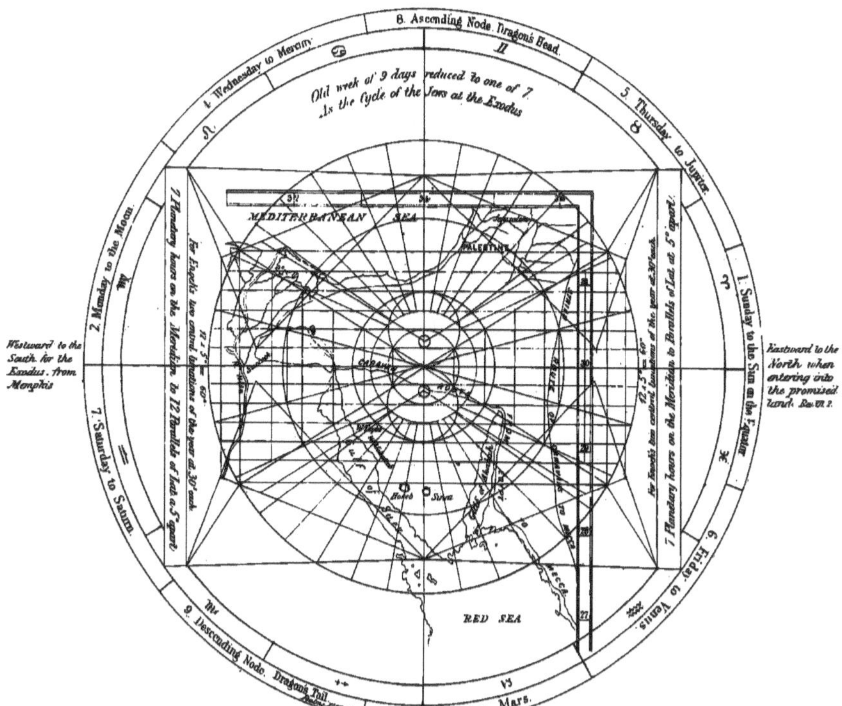
8. Ascending Node. Dragon's Head.
4. Wednesday to Mercury
5. Thursday to Jupiter
Old week of 9 days reduced to one of 7
As the Cycle of the Jews at the Exodus
2. Monday to the Moon.
1. Sunday to the Sun on the Equator
Westward to the South for the Exodus, from Memphis
Eastward to the North when entering into the promised land.
7 Planetary hours on the Meridian to 12 Parallels of Lat. a 5° apart.
For Enoch's two central luminaries of the year at 30° each
MEDITERRANEAN SEA
PALESTINE
Horeb
Sinai
RED SEA
7. Saturday to Saturn.
6. Friday to Venus.
9. Descending Node. Dragon's Tail
3. Tuesday to Mars.

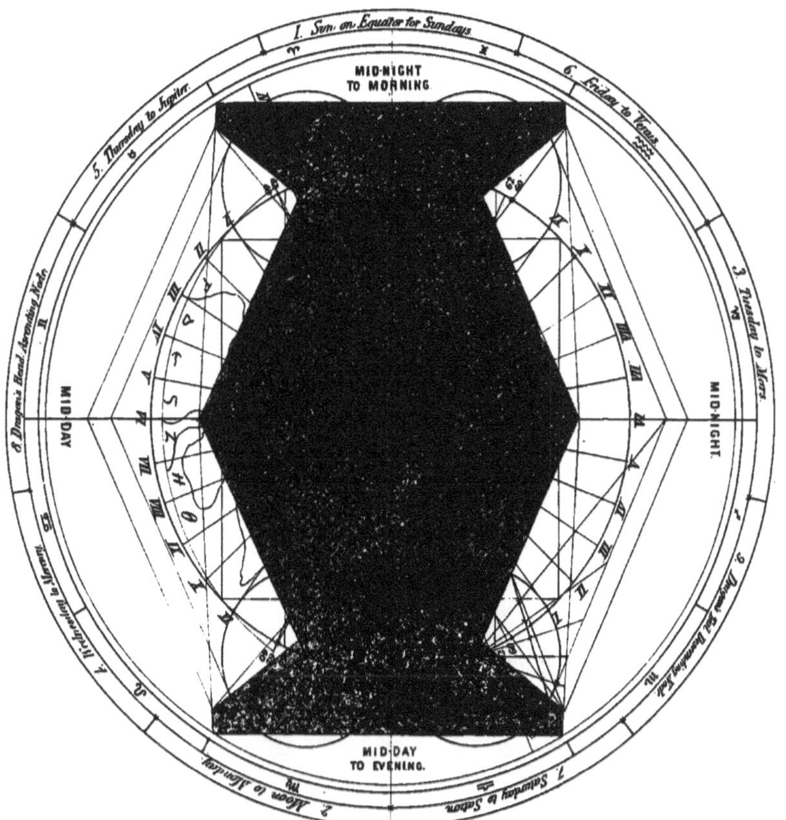

1. Sun on Equator for Sundays
MID-NIGHT
TO MORNING
6. Friday to Venus
5. Thursday to Jupiter
3. Tuesday to Mars
8. Dragon's Head Ascending Node
MID-DAY
MID-NIGHT
9. Dragon's Tail Descending Node
4. Wednesday to Mercury
MID-DAY
TO EVENING
2. Moon to Monday
7. Saturday to Saturn

The Hinder Zodiac for the Week of 8 Days, to the Lunar Cycle of 216 days of Years; as that of the 8 oldest Gods of Egypt, in the day's of Israel's captivity.

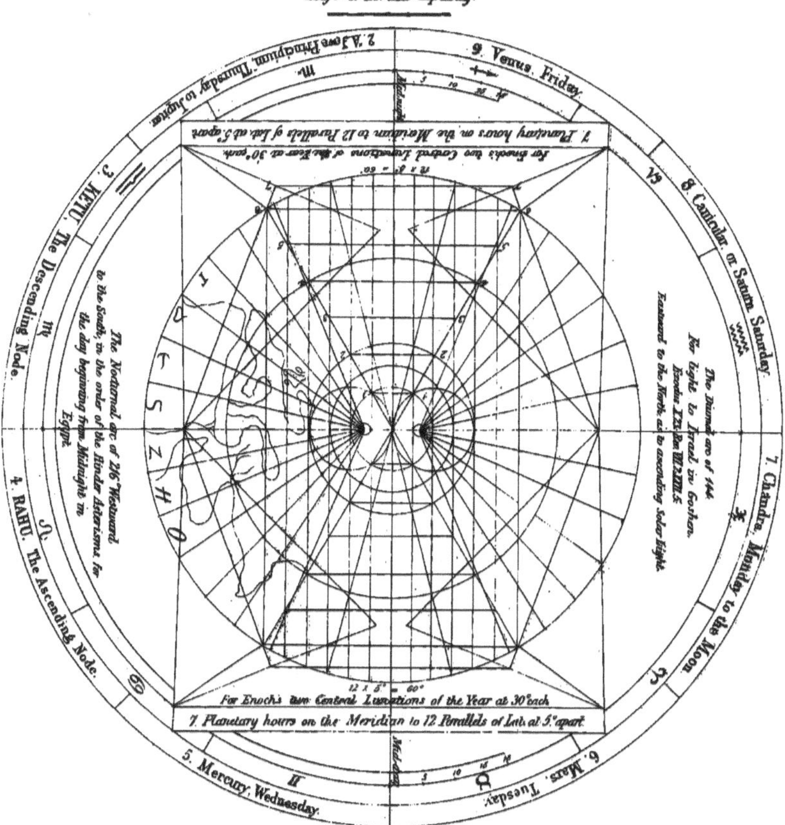

The middle curve represents the Equinoctial incline according to latitude. & divided into 12 equal parts.

Lines drawn, through these joints, from the centre to the Equinoctial, will determine the joints for the Hour lines on the upper & lower Curves.

The difference between the Diurnal arc on the Equator, & those for the longest & shortest days in N. Lat. 54 for Whitby, is nearly as that of Enochs Astronomy, in its relation to the Noahs Ark Dialling of antediluvian account for ancient Nineveh: viz. 60 degrees of the Equinoctial, or 4 hours of 15.° each.

This difference seems to have been measured to the twilight of typical time, by the "to & Fro" movements of the shadow over an arc of 60.° on the side steps of their typical dialling.

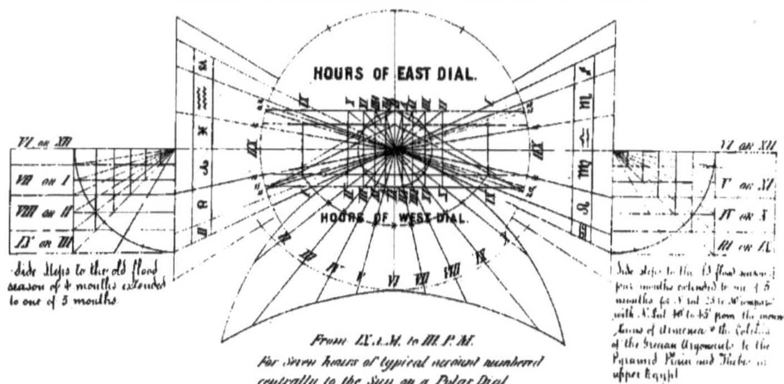

From IX A.M. to III P.M.

For seven hours of typical nercient numbered centrally to the Sun on a Polar Dial.

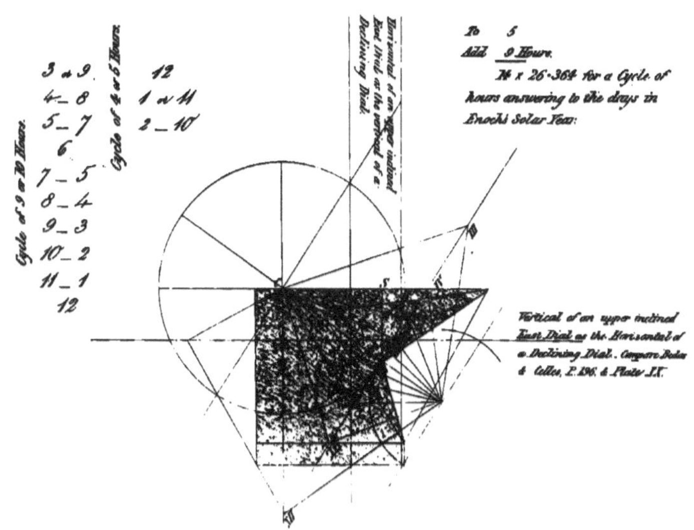
Cycle of 9 or 10 Hours.
3 or 9.
4 _ 8
5 _ 7
6
7 _ 5
8 _ 4
9 _ 3
10 _ 2
11 _ 1
12
Cycle of 4 or 5 Hours.
12
1 or 11
2 _ 10
Horizontal of an upper inclined East Dial as the vertical of a Declining Dial.
To 5
Add 9 Hours.
14 x 26 · 364 for a Cycle of hours answering to the days in Enochs Solar Year:
Vertical of an upper inclined East Dial as the Horizontal of a Declining Dial. Compare Bedos & Celles, P. 196. & Plate IX.

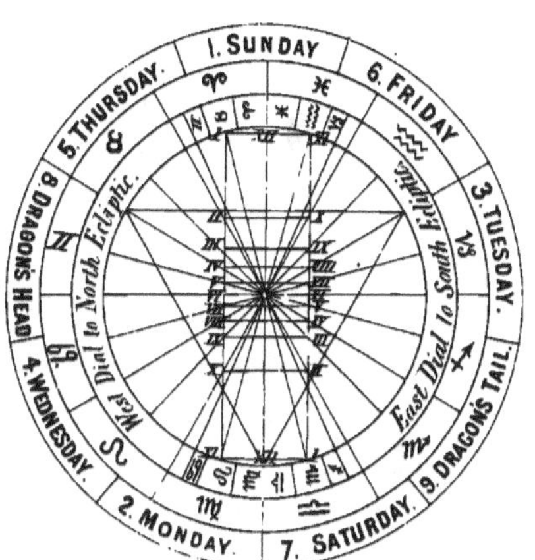
1. SUNDAY
6. FRIDAY
3. TUESDAY.
9. DRAGON'S TAIL.
7. SATURDAY.
2. MONDAY.
4. WEDNESDAY.
8. DRAGON'S HEAD
5. THURSDAY.
West Dial to North Ecliptic.
East Dial to South Ecliptic.

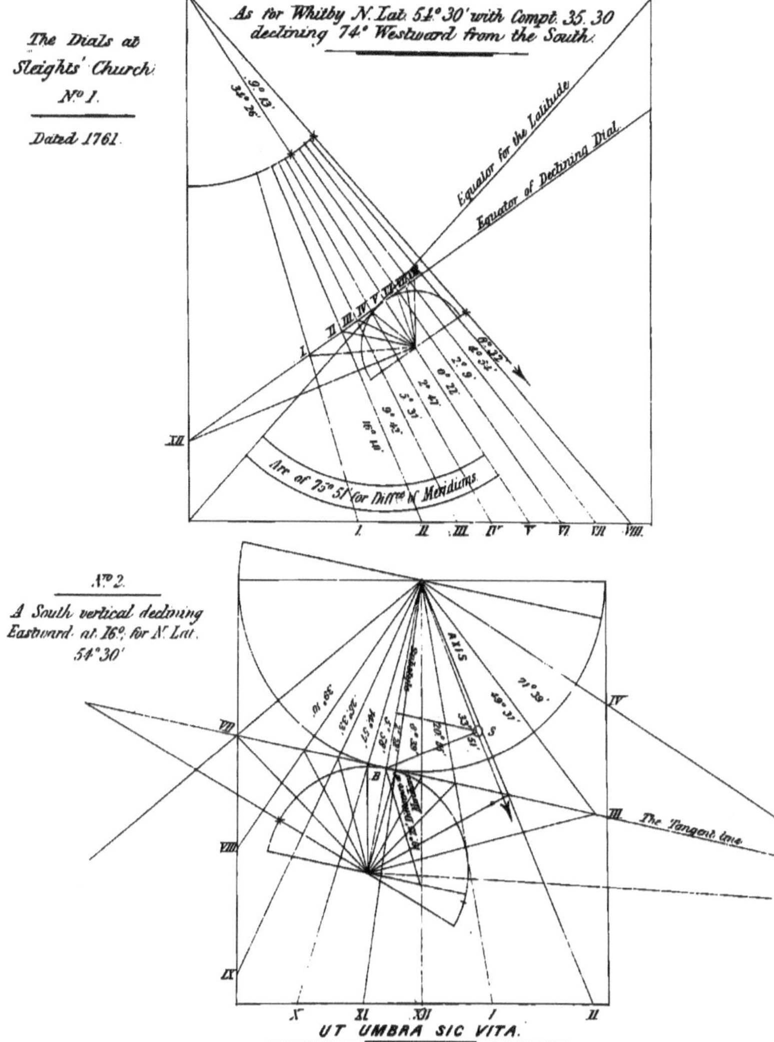

"Man's day" — as a passing shadow, — "the vapour" of James IV 14: John XI 9. Matt. XX 1: 6.

The Lofthouse Dial dated 1843 with Declination Eastward at 38° for inclination of Meridians at Arc 45° or 3 hours apart between London & Madagascar.

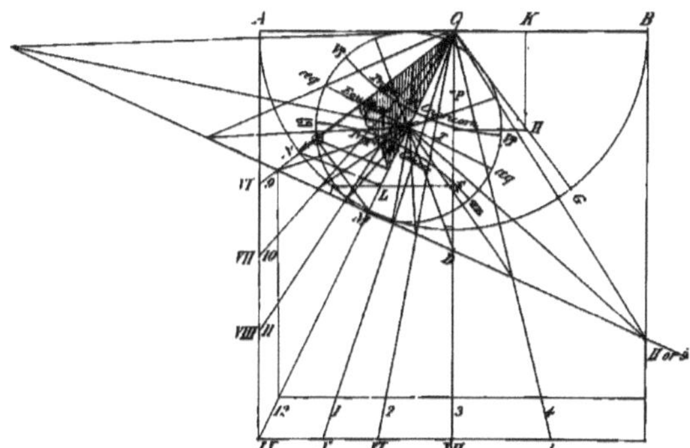

The Theatre at MACAO, from a *small* Photograph, purchased at an Exhibition in London of Chinese Scenery, at a Gallery of Water-coloured Paintings, by Hildebrandt, *circa* 1865, in Pall Mall.

THE WINGED DISC; OR, SERAPHIC EMBLEM OF THE ANCIENT EGYPTIANS

To the Meridian of their East and West Typical Dialling, compared with Piazzi Smyth's meridian section of the Great Pyramid.

On this typical division of the Ecliptic Northward and Southward to the East and West, compare Gen. iii. 24 with Zech. xiv. 4, on the Mount of Olives, which is before Jerusalem *on the East*, being similarly typified to the "Advent of Messiah, as the SUN of Righteousness."

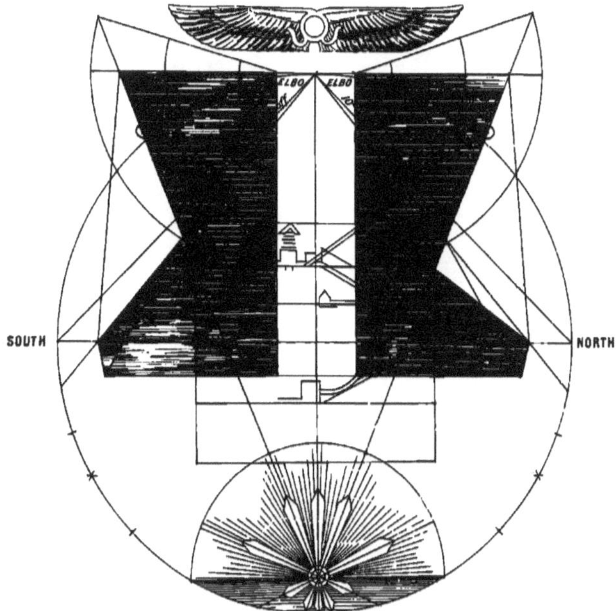

The fiery sword which turned every way to guard (as unto God) the way of the Tree of Life given to the intersection of the Equator by Earth's Axis, in the four Quadrants of their East and West Dialling.

The decorated cross of the Anglican-Church Calender, as the fiery sword of Gen. iii. over the Cherubim guarding the way of the Tree of Life.

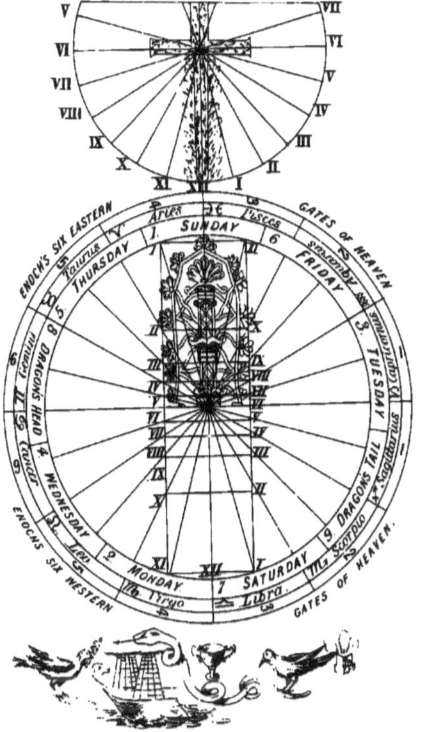

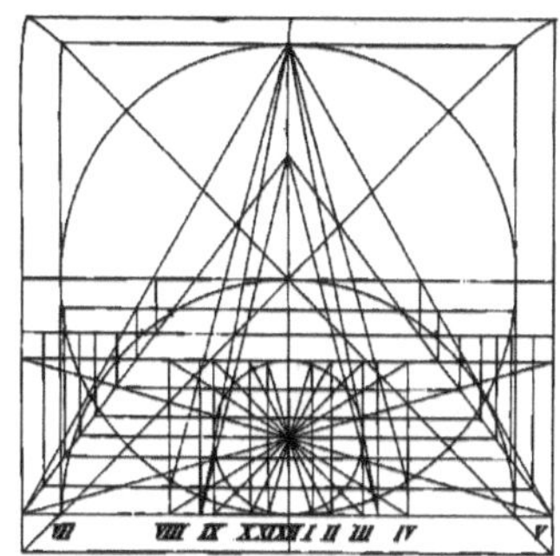

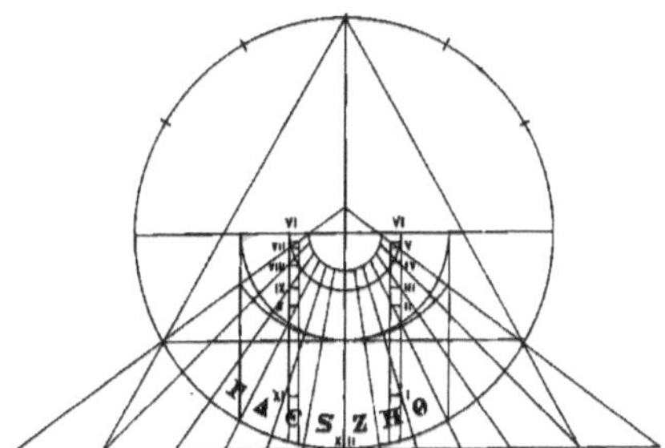

West Side of a Dial for N. Lat. 54°, constructed like the Greek-Egyptian Dial with Steps.

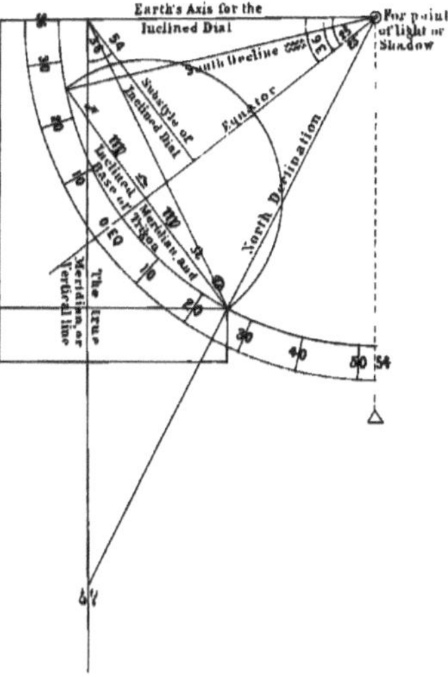

FOR THE EXHIBITION TRACT.

The Alexandrine Dial verified, *definitively*, on the Scale of the Model made for me by Mr A. HAYES of the British Museum.

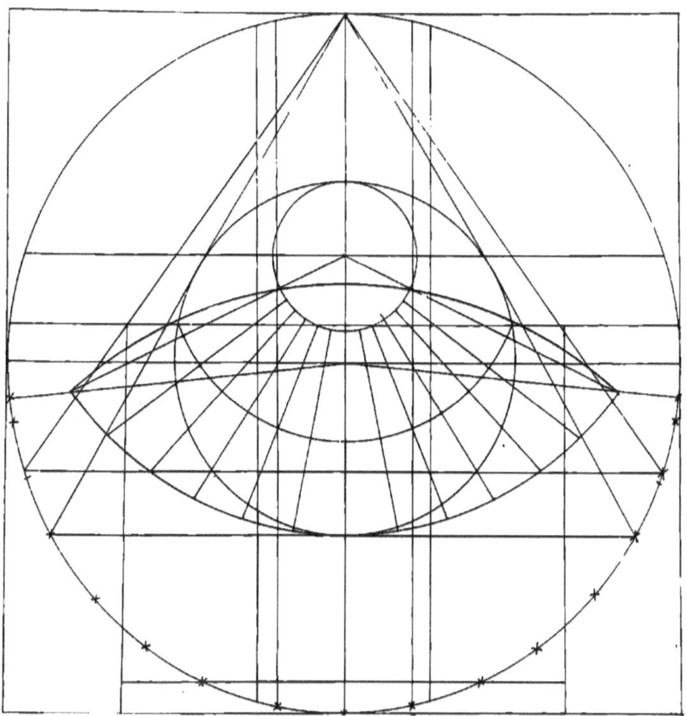

THE MERIDIAN OF A DECLINING SOUTH VERTICAL DIAL,

Divided to the Sun's North Declination, as on the Seven Steps of the Greek-Egyptian Dial.

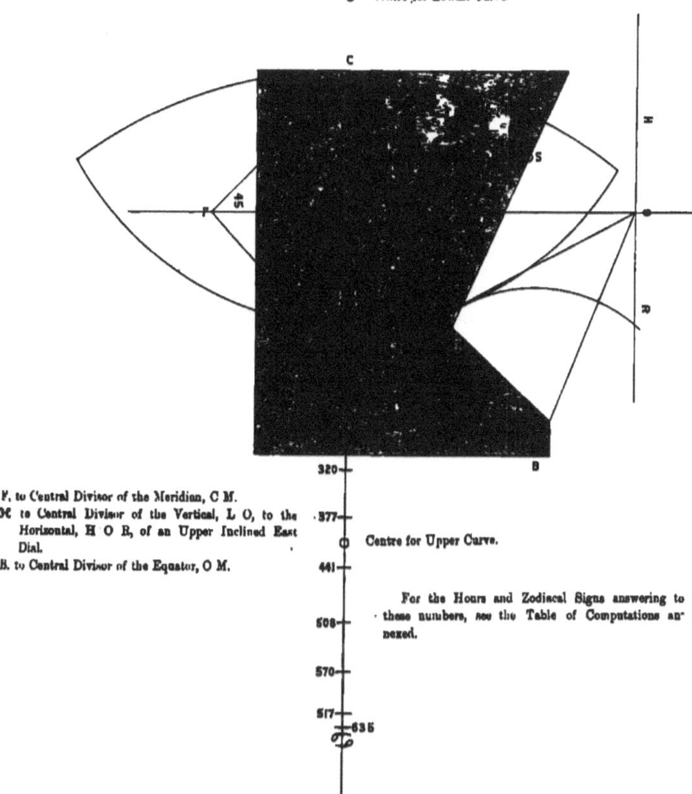

MEDEA D'ARLES

THE PLANETARY AND EQUINOCTIAL DIALLING HOURS OF THE GREEK-EGYPTIAN DIAL, WITH STEPS,

Proved to be in Harmony with its typical design, as long since ascertained in itself, though only thus brought into harmony with exact dialling laws.

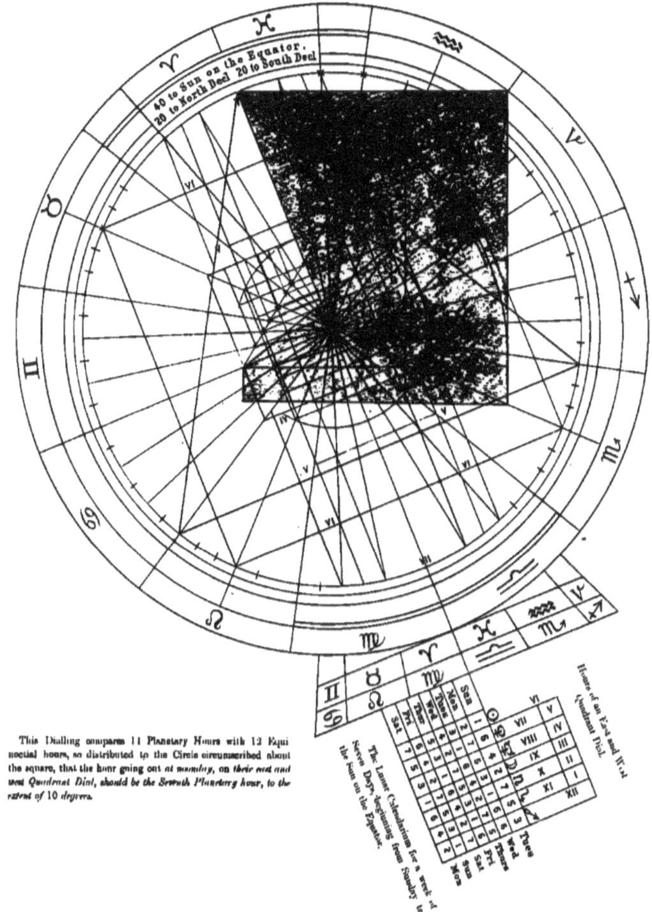

This Dialling compares 11 Planetary Hours with 12 Equinoctial hours, so distributed to the Circle circumscribed about the square, that the hour going out *at noonday*, on *their east and west Quadrant Dial, should be the Seventh Planetary hour, to the extent of* 10 *degrees.*

N.B.—These Planetary Hours seem to have been taken (as above) on the Tangent line of 15°, as a mean between those of 10 and 20 degrees of Radius of the Hour Circle.

Note also that (according to the testimony of Dr Rieu, keeper of the Sanscrit MSS., in the British Museum) Vishnu was worshipped in the month *Sravana* (when the Sun was in Cancer, and yet in some way connected with *triangulum above Aries*, as TRIVIKRUM, or the *three stepper*), as then their divider of months and years into *three* instead of four seasons.

The interlacing of the two aquatic plants of Egypt, depicted on the thrones of the Pharaohs, holds among the Egyptians the same rank and importance that *the symbolic* Tree of Life at Khorsabad does among the Assyrians. (See Bonomi, p. 160, and compare Rev. xxii. 1, 2, for the relation of the River of Life to the meridian on the East and West Dialling of the Ancient Orientals.)

The Lotus on symbol *neb.* Lord was the national emblem of Upper Egypt (Bunson, vol. 1, p. 522)

Papyrus plants on symbol of land, or in a pool, were the emblem of Lower Egypt and the Delta.

(?) The Janus of the Egyptians, for the beginning of their year southward at the winter tropic, as we calendar the year on our Dials by the Trigon.—*Copied from Osborne's "Monumental Egypt,"* vol. ii., p. 75.

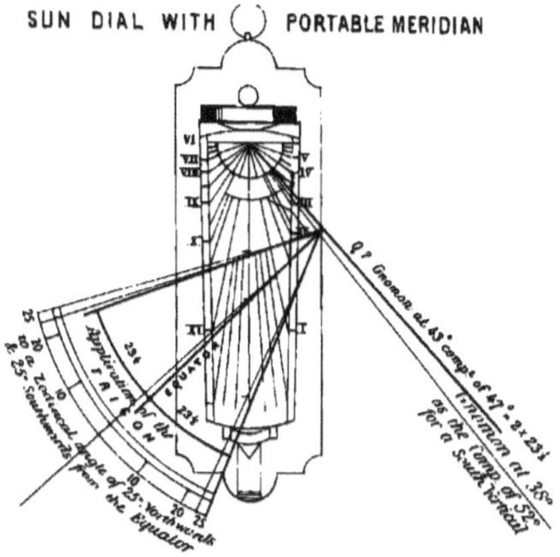

43° is the angle of the Gnomon on Blackie's diagram, if correct. But whether the copy of an antique, or (as I at first supposed) a south vertical for London, there is no evidence to shew; unless the angle of 43° for the Gnomon should indicate a form of the quadrant universal dial.

Thus, one latitude marking on the Alexandrine Dial is clearly 40°, the complement of 50°; or of 2 × 25°, the then zodiacal angle.

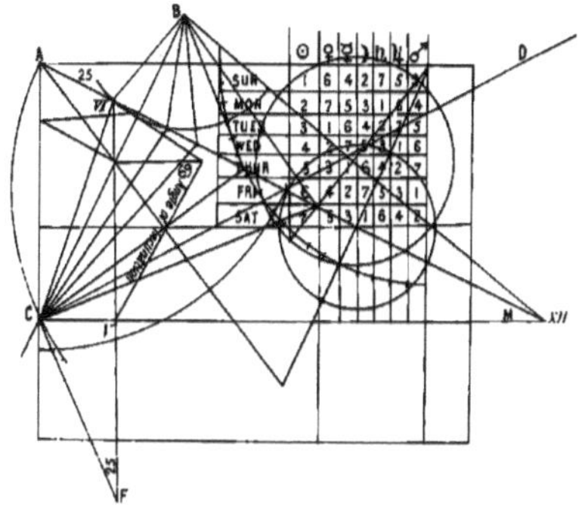
A
B
C
D
F
M
XII
25
SUN
MON
FRI
SAT

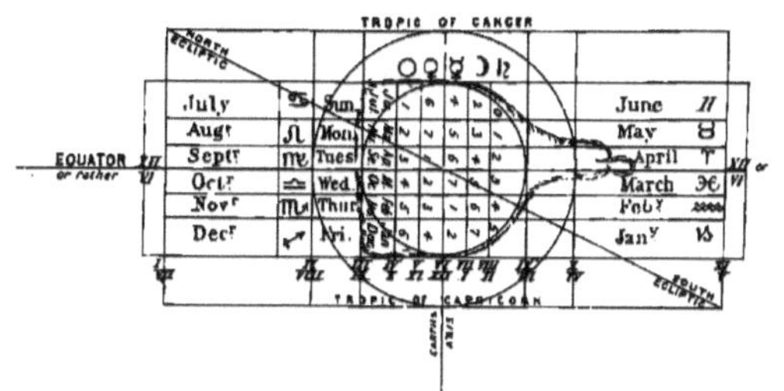

TROPIC OF CANCER
NORTH ECLIPTIC
July
Augt
Septr
Octr
Novr
Decr
June
May
April
March
Feby
Jany
EQUATOR
or rather
SOUTH ECLIPTIC
TROPIC OF CAPRICORN

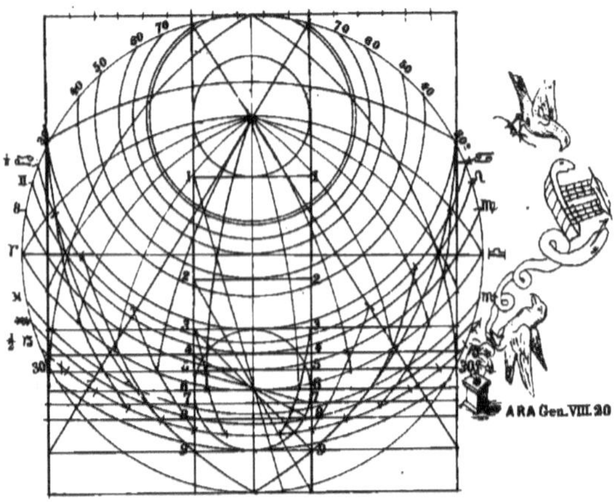

The Hollow Horizontal Dial of the Ancients (from Fale's Dialling, black-lettered, London, A.D. 1593, *printed (viz., the copy to which reference is made) by Felix Kingstone, dwelling in Pater Noster Row,* 1652*) in its relation to the Greek-Egyptian Dial with Steps.*

This is here presumed to represent the ancient "*Scaphe*, or *Boat-Dial*" of the Noah's ark symbolism, though (to the best of my knowledge) we have no evidence of its exact form handed down to us, like that of the "Shield-Dial" discovered in the ruins of Herculaneum.

www.ingramcontent.com/pod-product-compliance
Lightning Source LLC
Chambersburg PA
CBHW032110230426
43672CB00009B/1691

* 9 7 8 3 3 3 7 2 4 3 2 1 0 *